Careers in
Specialized Consulting:
Health Care, Human Resources,
and Information Technology

2007 Edition

WetFeet Insider Guide

Helping you make smarter career decisions.

WetFeet, Inc.

The Folger Building
101 Howard Street
Suite 300
San Francisco, CA 94105

Phone: (415) 284-7900 or 1-800-926-4JOB
Fax: (415) 284-7910
Website: www.wetfeet.com

Careers in Specialized Consulting:
Health Care, Human Resources, and Information Technology

2007 Edition
ISBN: 978-1-58207-678-2

Table of Contents

Specialized Consulting at a Glance

Opportunity Overview

- Human resources, IT, and health care consultants are hired by large, diversified consulting firms with multiple practices and by specialized firms that focus on one type of consulting.

- As a general rule, firms that specialize in a specific industry or function hire fewer candidates directly from undergraduate or MBA programs than strategy firms (unless they offer relevant industry or function experience).

- Consultants who have earned MBA or JD (law) degrees are more common in strategy consulting than in human resources or IT consulting. Many health care consulting firms court professionals with multiple advanced degrees, such as MDs, MBAs, and PhDs, as well as advanced public policy degrees.

- Human resources, IT, and health care consulting firms, in comparison to strategy firms, hire more experienced, midcareer professionals on an ad hoc basis into various levels of their organizations.

Advantages of a Career in Specialized Consulting

- It's an excellent opportunity to build expertise in a specific industry or function while learning how companies operate.

- The field attracts talented, fun, hardworking people.

- An MBA (or other advanced degree) is not always de rigueur for career advancement.

- Smaller, more specialized consulting firms often allow you to assume greater responsibility and pursue a more flexible career path than larger firms do.

- If you love to travel, this career may satisfy your wanderlust, and if you adore the amenities of posh hotels, you might just find yourself in your element.

Disadvantages of a Career in Specialized Consulting

- You will often be asked to work relatively long, unpredictable work hours (55 to 60 per week on average)—regardless of your industry or functional specialty.

- Depending on the specific firm, you may not enjoy the same name-brand recognition and instant cachet as your counterparts in strategy consulting.

- As is the case in all service industries, your life's not your own—it belongs to your clients.

- You're a few steps removed from actual decision-making and profit/loss responsibility. Consultants can only make suggestions; there's no guarantee that they'll be successfully implemented. This can be frustrating.

- Lots and lots of travel: If you don't enjoy airports or you want to sit down to dinner every night with your family, this may not be the career path for you.

Recruiting Overview

- Some firms hire consultants directly into industry or function-specific areas of expertise, while others hire generalists who may choose to specialize later in their careers.

- While many firms recruit on campus, smaller firms often don't maintain highly visible, formal recruiting campaigns.

- Lateral and midcareer hires are more common in specialized consulting than in strategy consulting.

- Academic and analytical abilities as well as relevant professional experience are emphasized.

- Case interviews are mandatory for most firms (and can be agonizing for the unprepared).

What Recruiters Look For

- When evaluating resumes, consulting recruiters typically look for evidence of communication skills, quantitative aptitude, leadership ability, and academic achievement. Many firms—especially smaller, more specialized firms—also look for relevant experience (or a clearly demonstrated interest) in the particular industry or function in which the firm specializes.

- In the interview, the recruiter wants to know how a candidate thinks. Interviewees are encouraged to be themselves, to answer questions directly and honestly, and to verbalize thoughts comprehensively and succinctly.

- Recruiters agree that students who succeed in consulting have strong problem-solving skills, work well in teams, and share a commitment to help clients.

The Industry

Introduction

These days, it seems like everyone you meet is a consultant. Personal trainers are "health and fitness consultants." The guy behind the counter at your local Kinko's is an "image reproduction consultant." The kid who cuts your lawn is a "landscaping consultant."

The term *consulting* is often used as a one-size-fits-all term for virtually any form of organizational advice-giving. WetFeet's Insider Guide to *Careers in Management Consulting* focuses on the variety known as *strategy consulting*. Dominated by firms such as McKinsey & Company, Bain & Company, the Boston Consulting Group, and Booz Allen Hamilton, strategy consulting firms enjoy the most immediate brand-name recognition in both corporate and consulting circles. They conduct highly visible and painstakingly formal recruiting at the most prestigious undergraduate institutions and MBA programs worldwide, and these firms enjoy the luxury of choosing from the intellectual elite at each school. In terms of new hires, strategy firms have both quality and quantity on their side. Because of the size and scope of their consulting practices, they can hire—and train—a considerable number of undergraduates and new MBAs year after year.

Although the top firms in this category perpetuate a cult-like fascination with the profession among consulting hopefuls, strategy consulting actually represents only one slice of the consulting pie. There are other types of consulting, too. This guide focuses on three: human resources (HR), information technology (IT), and health care consulting.

Why these three? Two of them—HR and IT—represent functional specialties that are relevant and valuable to virtually any company, regardless of its sector, industry, geographical location, or competitive position. The third—health care consulting—represents a category defined along industry (rather than functional) lines. While HR and IT consultants serve clients in a range of industries, health care consultants (as their name implies) advise hospitals, medical schools, pharmaceutical companies, and other health care organizations on a range of issues (both strategic and operational) unique to their industry. Though consulting practices have sprung up to serve other industries as well (financial services, retail, and consumer packaged goods, just to name a few), we've chosen to highlight health care consulting because (compared to other industry-specific consulting practices) it represents a more sizeable revenue-generating opportunity for larger, diversified strategy firms as well as smaller, more specialized consulting shops.

Whether you've got your heart set on one particular functional or industry specialty or you're just beginning to consider how to embark on a more specialized consulting track, this guide will provide you with an overview of what it's like to work in HR, IT, and health care consulting. You will also learn how these three types of work fit into the larger consulting picture. In these pages, we'll describe different projects that our consulting insiders have worked on in the HR, IT, and health care arenas. We'll let you know what economic trends will affect business (and career) opportunities in each consulting realm, and which trends you should know about—well in advance of your interviews. Of course, we'll also identify firms that offer particularly strong consulting practices in one or more of these practice areas, and outline the recruiting process followed by most consulting firms in these sectors. As always, we'll provide insiders' perspectives on their careers and respective organizations.

Consulting Overview

If you've done a little bit of homework on consulting careers so far—even if your research to date has only involved speaking to classmates who've just gotten started along the consulting path—you know that many companies are willing to part with serious cash for an objective, trustworthy counselor. Indeed, consulting firms may charge their clients anywhere from $300,000 to $1 million in monthly fees, billing $5,000 a day for top consultants and $1,500 for their associates—plus expenses, of course.

How can consulting firms justify these stratospheric fees, and, moreover, how can client organizations justify paying them? Essentially, clients pay consultants for their institutional knowledge and accumulated wisdom: expertise they've developed by providing guidance to other organizations on similar issues. Consulting firms are knowledge organizations with economies of scale on their side: They can cultivate expertise at a level that's usually not economical within a particular company. For example, protecting the security of an organization's computing systems requires a high level of specialized expertise. By providing advisory services to many organizations, a firm that provides consulting on computer security issues can achieve the necessary "critical mass" to fully develop its expertise in such a highly nuanced area.

Many companies—particularly Fortune 500 companies—call on external consultants even though they have internal consultants on the payroll, because it turns out to be more economical. External consultants generally tackle issues with which the client has little prior experience, or they handle projects for which the client has insufficient in-house capability. One-time, resource-intensive projects such as reorganizing a company after a merger, or launching a new customer relationship management system to leverage point-of-sale data—these are the types of initiatives for which a company is likely to enlist a consultant. Since it would be impractical to keep such specialized knowledge in-house for a one-time project, companies may find it more economical to outsource these projects to outside firms.

Despite the seemingly exorbitant fees they charge the companies they advise, consulting firms provide critical services to their clients and deliver measurable results. Though a company might bear a significant expense to retain a consulting firm to help with a post-merger systems integration, for example, it would probably cost that company even more if it attempted the implementation on its own and made costly mistakes along the way. Not only do consultants often preempt expensive snafus when an organization attempts a significant change, they also offer fresh, objective perspectives, as well as data and market intelligence that an individual organization would have difficulty obtaining on its own. Because they offer targeted experience across multiple clients and engagements, consultants offer their clients the processes and human resources capabilities that implement change more smoothly than they otherwise would. Clients also value consultants' (relative) objectivity and immunity from internal politics: Unlike a company's own leadership, consultants can recommend the best course of action for a company without worrying about whether their decision will be unpopular.

On the downside, consultants are often asked to make difficult decisions and deliver unpleasant news in the event of a cost-cutting initiative or downsizing. Clients can use consultants as a front for cost-cutting or layoffs, and ask them to make these changes as well (remember the Bobs in the movie *Office Space*?). Consultants are far more eager to shepherd companies through periods of rapid growth and economic expansion than they are to do the dirty work that comes along with recessions and downsizing. For better or for worse, consultants are in demand during the highs and lows of the economic cycle, and all points in between.

Hiring Outlook

After several down years, firms began recruiting in earnest again in 2004. In 2005, consulting firm recruiting was up 30 to 50 percent ("Consulting Firms Court New M.B.A. Recruits," *Wall Street Journal*, 2/8/05)—and the hiring outlook remains bright in 2006. According to one insider, "We see a movement upward in the number of hiring. We're seeing a lot more deals, and our capacity is at the highest mark that it's been in a couple of years. The management team absolutely thinks the work will continue."

Consulting has, again, become a hot ticket for undergraduates and MBAs. Although the general mood among recruiters would be better described as cautious optimism rather than irrational exuberance, insiders report that recruiting is up at the larger firms and stable at boutique shops. "Hiring has definitely increased from [the early 2000s]. With our market picking up with the economy, that's had ripple effects," says a recruiting insider.

Much of the turbulence that characterized the industry in the early part of the decade has quieted down. Deloitte Consulting is now squarely back in the Deloitte Touche Tohmatsu fold after its aborted spinoff attempt in 2003, and PwC Consulting became part of IBM after its 2002 sale to Big Blue. With much of the uncertainty within individual consulting companies resolved, the nebulous, wait-and-see attitude toward hiring has turned into a solid hiring program.

Still, the growth that appears to have begun won't mirror that of the go-go 1990s. "I don't think we'll see the spike in growth that we saw in the late '90s," says an insider. "We moved through the early 2000s on cost reduction. Now the focus is on growth of the bottom line. The focus isn't so much on how fast I can grow my top line or how I can cut my costs, but how I can improve my productivity. I think those initiatives are going to drive the opportunities for growth in the consulting industry."

Other things have changed since the 1990s, as well. For one thing, because clients' buying patterns with consulting services are continually fluctuating, firms are looking for more professional work experience in those they hire. "What I've been seeing is that the buyers (clients) are looking for less hype and more substance," an insider says. "Over the boom years, there were a lot of high-flying firms with a lot of hype around them; now what we're seeing is a buying community that's a little more savvy, a little more senior. Recruiting decisions are being moved up higher in the organization."

"For the pre-MBA experience, it would be advantageous to make sure they're getting some serious, substantial experience—industry experience for the type of client engagements they want to work in post-MBA," an insider says. "Some MBAs will look at the summer associate program as an opportunity to try something completely different. But if they're trying something for variety, and they want to work in a post-MBA position in a field different than their summer position, they're putting themselves at a disadvantage."

The Breakdown: Navigating the Consulting Maze

As we've said, consultants (and consulting firms) come in many different flavors. Strategy consulting—traditionally dominated by the heavy hitters of the consulting league, such as McKinsey, Bain, and the Boston Consulting Group—focuses on the organization-wide issues that occupy the minds of a company's CEO and senior-most management. Strategy consulting engagements span sectors, industries, and disciplines, but the common denominator that distinguishes strategic consulting from other types of consulting is its *external* focus: Strategy consulting examines how an organization can meet its objectives given its customers, competitors, suppliers, and the broader industry-wide and economy-wide trends that affect its business.

In contrast, consultants aligned with a particular functional area (e.g., human resources or IT) spend most of their time examining their clients' *internal* processes to help the company operate more effectively or efficiently. Like their counterparts in strategy consulting, these consultants serve clients across various sectors and industries, utilizing the depth of their talent management or technical expertise across client companies. Rather than shaping their clients' organizational strategy, operations consultants support it by helping their clients leverage a given internal function or process to its full potential. For instance, a human resources consulting firm enlisted to redesign a company's performance management system is essentially examining how the company can improve an internal process. By improving its own promotion and compensation policies, the company will be better equipped to retain the most talented people. In turn, the company is better prepared to meet its strategic objectives. Consultants specializing in a given function typically work with the company's leadership in the corresponding functional area; for example, HR consultants would likely work more closely with the company's VP of HR and those who report directly to him or her.

Consultants who specialize in a particular industry (e.g., health care) are a different type of animal. Health care consultants may tackle any type of engagement—strategic, operational, or otherwise—with an eye toward the issues that are unique to players in the health care industry. Health care consulting (as are its counterparts in the field of financial services or consumer packaged goods) is often referred to as a *vertical practice area* (as opposed to a *horizontal practice area*). A vertical consulting practice offers a general management consultancy applicable to one industry only, whereas a horizontal consulting practice (e.g., HR or IT) focuses on a specific discipline applicable to many different industries.

If you think you've got it straight so far, rest assured that things are about to get a little hairier. First of all, it's worth mentioning that all consulting assignments—regardless of the client or the consulting firm—represent a point on the spectrum from operational to strategic thinking. A retail company, for example, might hire a consulting firm to investigate whether there's a link between employee attrition and lagging sales in one of its store locations. A year later, that same retail company (hopefully with happier employees and more robust sales numbers) may hire a consulting firm to administer the benefits program for employees in all of its stores. Both of these assignments may officially fall within the scope of HR consulting, but the employee retention issue represents a strategic priority, whereas the benefits administration engagement is an operational one.

To further complicate things, some of the largest strategy players have developed dedicated practice areas targeted toward specific industries and functions. The Boston Consulting Group, for example, offers an information technology practice, a human resources practice (called "Organization"), and a health care vertical. In fact, both BCG and McKinsey appear on the list of top-ten health care consulting practices by revenue, even though both would (rightly) eschew classification as health care consulting firms.

Typically, the functional practice lines at strategy firms tend to focus on the strategic issues (rather than the operational issues) associated with that function. For example,

BCG might help an organization determine that its ineffective compensation processes are inhibiting its ability to retain key senior talent; however, it typically would not prescribe or implement a specific online performance appraisal system to remedy the problem. An HR consulting firm such as the Hay Group, on the other hand, might diagnose the performance-management problem *and* treat it by prescribing its proprietary compensation-benchmarking tool. Though a strategy firm and a dedicated HR consulting firm may offer their clients different core competencies, it's worth pointing out that they can (and often do) compete with each other for consulting engagements. This is true in IT and health care consulting, as well.

In addition, a consulting industry–wide trend toward consolidation makes classification among the consulting ranks an even thornier issue. As consulting firms scramble to provide clients (and prospective clients) with "one-stop shopping" for their strategic and operational needs, many of the larger players have been courting smaller, more specialized practices that complement or enhance their own portfolio of services. In the past few years, firms such as IBM and Hewitt have pursued and landed certain strategic acquisitions in order to gain entry into particular industries or functional areas or to provide "end-to-end" services to their clients. In the past, consulting firms faced seemingly impenetrable boundaries designating where one firm's strategic advisory work ended and another firm's implementation work began. In today's competitive landscape, many consulting behemoths have gained considerable market share through a different approach: providing a greater range of services to clients, thereby extending the longevity—and potential profitability—of each client engagement.

The "Big O": Business Process Outsourcing

Of the trends shaping the demand for HR and IT consulting services in particular, the shift toward business process outsourcing (BPO) is perhaps the most significant. Outsourcing represents the biggest single growth opportunity for many business-services firms. According to Gartner research, BPO is an approximately $300 billion market in its own right, and it will only gain momentum over the next few years. According to an insider, "Outsourcing is growing, and not going to go away."

So what exactly is BPO? As the name suggests, business process outsourcing is the contracting of a specific business task to a third-party service provider. Usually, BPO is implemented as a cost-saving measure for tasks that a company requires but does not depend on to maintain its position in the marketplace. If companies can outsource their non-core operations to an outside provider (who can most likely provide these services more efficiently and cost-effectively), they can focus on the issues intrinsic to their business. Popular candidates for outsourcing include finance, human resources, employee training, procurement, and logistics. Though it is sometimes lumped into the larger BPO umbrella, IT outsourcing accounts for such a substantial proportion of total outsourcing revenue that it's typically afforded its own category.

BPO isn't a new concept, or a new trend. The underlying logic behind BPO is the same logic that convinces many time-starved professionals to send their laundry out to be washed and folded by someone else: Sure, they could do it themselves—and it might even be a little bit cheaper if they did—but by the time you factor in the precious free time they'd sacrifice in the process, it makes far more sense for them to pay 90 cents per pound and be done with it. It's no different on a corporate scale: Rather than fussing about with defined benefit and defined contribution plans, health insurance schemes, and payroll, many companies prefer to outsource these processes to outside vendors. In fact, companies may extend their reliance on BPO well past the boundaries of one or two individual processes; it's not unheard of, for example, for a firm to conduct an HR "lift and shift," outsourcing its entire human resources department to a third-party vendor.

Many of the larger HR consultancies (e.g., Hewitt, Towers Perrin, and Mercer) derive a significant percentage of their revenue from precisely this sort of work.

Likewise, virtually all of the IT consulting heavy hitters (e.g., IBM, Accenture, Capgemini, and CSC) rely on their sizeable technology outsourcing practices to buoy their revenue growth, especially when revenues in their consulting practices lag. Not only do many consulting firms win billions of dollars doing this type of work, they can also take advantage of the ample cross-selling opportunities to expand their consulting businesses. As one insider put it, "It's a lot easier to sell consulting services to a client if you've already gotten your foot in the door with outsourcing work."

IMPLICATIONS FOR CONSULTING

So what does all of this mean for the consulting industry? And what does it mean for the HR and IT consulting segments in particular? For one thing, it becomes more and more difficult to distinguish the top firms from each other based on revenue alone. Consulting and outsourcing—though they are often lumped together under the term "business services" on the firm's income statement—are two very different value propositions for the client (not to mention two very different types of work for the job seeker). As consulting firms generate more and more revenue from their outsourcing practices, the competitive landscape for consulting services becomes more complex. Consider the HR consulting market, for example: In one sense, the popularity of BPO is good news for the HR consulting firms that offer outsourcing services. The more HR processes their clients decide to outsource, the greater the revenue stream they can generate from their relationships with these clients. But for traditional HR consulting firms, the market's emphasis on BPO is a double-edged sword; one by one, firms that have traditionally not been heavy hitters in the HR consulting world have been getting in on the outsourcing action, stealing market share from the larger, more established HR service providers. Firms such as IBM, EDS, and CSC are among the largest providers of IT and business-process outsourcing services, and they're giving the pure-play HR outsourcers a run for their money.

Not only has the expansion of the BPO market meant more competition for consulting firms, it has indirectly launched a different type of consulting opportunity for strategic consulting firms such as McKinsey, Bain, and BCG. Although firms in this category do not themselves act as third-party providers of business processes, they may advise companies on issues related to BPO; they may help a client company think about how to select vendors, how to negotiate pricing, and how to manage relationships with third-party providers. Regardless of the specific process that clients outsource—whether it's related to human resources, information technology, logistics, or facilities management—the strategy behind outsourcing is similar. As such, pure-play strategy consultancies have capitalized on their own revenue-generating opportunity by offering frameworks for addressing their clients' BPO strategies.

It's also worth pointing out that while outsourcing provides stable margins, it doesn't necessarily create more jobs for consultants. Even though firms may offer both types of services, outsourcing is nonetheless seen as a substitute for—rather than a driver of—consulting growth. Whenever a company outsources a business process, it's unlikely that the same business will hire a consultant to further improve that process. So, the current dominance of outsourcing is causing the most anxiety among more traditional consulting practices, which stand to lose a significant amount of market share to their hybrid cousins.

IMPLICATIONS FOR ASPIRING CONSULTANTS

So what does all of this mean for you, the jobseeker? It means there's a lot of information to keep straight as you assess which subset of consulting—and which particular firm—is the best match for you. If you've read the WetFeet Insider Guide to *Careers in Management Consulting*, you've probably concluded (correctly) that many management consulting firms provide comparable services to their clients, with a few variations in specialty and corporate culture. As you read this guide, you'll notice that this terrain is a little bit more uneven.

An HR consulting firm, for example, doesn't just hire HR consultants. Depending on whether it offers outsourcing, it may also hire armies of IT consultants to build and maintain systems for clients with which it has outsourcing contracts. That same HR consultancy may also hire health care consultants to examine ways of designing more cost-effective health care plans for employees, but these are not the same health care consultants who provide strategy, human resources, or IT advice to pharmaceutical companies. In this guide, *health care consultant* refers to people who work for health care consulting practices, which may operate independently, within an industry group at a strategy firm, or within a diversified Big Four consultancy that also offers IT and HR practices. At larger firms, there will be legions of IT consultants, aligned with health care practices, HR practices, and (you guessed it) technology practices. Is your head spinning yet? (Ours are.) Don't worry; we'll walk you through all of this information step by step.

Though it seems daunting to keep track of who does what and in what context, it's imperative that you *do* keep track, especially if you want to set yourself apart during the notoriously rigorous recruiting process. If you've set your sights on a specific subset of the consulting arena, it's simply not enough to establish your raw intellectual horse-power, capacity for problem solving, and willingness to trot the globe to solve your clients' most pressing business challenges. You must also know (and be able to articulate) what you find compelling about a given industry or function and what macro and micro trends characterize that particular space. Not only that, it's important to demon-strate that you've fueled your passion for HR (or IT or health care) consulting with substantial research. If you can prove to your interviewer that you've not only got what it takes to flourish as a consultant, but that you've gone the extra mile to learn what kind of consulting you'd like to do (and what distinguishes one consulting practice from another), you'll be well on your way to a lifetime of frequent flier miles.

Rank and File

The consulting industry doesn't lend itself to easy numerical comparisons. First, many firms are privately held, so revenue and profit figures aren't readily available. Second, there is considerable disagreement over what constitutes consulting revenue. Are we to consider all of the fee income or management consulting revenue only? How do we handle firms that have several different business units that provide consulting? Third, as we've noted, many firms tend to operate in a variety of sectors, from outsourcing to IT to strategy, which makes it challenging to classify industry players. For instance, it's clear that McKinsey is a management consulting firm, but what about IBM, which has a large systems consulting group? All this is to say that you should pick your target firms based on what *you* are looking for in your consulting career and where you think you'll fit in best.

The rankings below are from an annual survey of MBAs who named the companies they'd most like to work for in 2005 and *Consulting Magazine*'s list of top firms to work for.

WHERE MBAS WANT TO WORK

Consulting Firms that Ranked in the Top 100

Rank	Firm
1	McKinsey & Company
4	Bain & Company
5	The Boston Consulting Group
15	Booz Allen Hamilton
17	Deloitte*
23	IBM**
43	Accenture
63	A.T. Kearney
68	Monitor Group
78	Mercer Management Consulting
100	BearingPoint

*Includes consulting and audit units.
**Includes IBM Global Services.
Source: *Fortune*'s 2006 "100 Top MBA Employers" list

10 Best Consulting Firms to Work For, Listed Alphabetically

Bain & Co.
Booz Allen Hamilton
Boston Consulting Group
DiamondCluster International
Kurt Salmon Associates
McKinsey & Company
Mercer Management Consulting
Mercer Oliver Wyman
Pittaglio Rabin Todd & McGrath
Sapient*

*Ranked first overall in survey.
Source: *Consulting Magazine*, August 2005

The Consulting Sectors

Health Care Consulting

Human Resources Consulting

Information Technology/Systems Consulting

Picking and Choosing

Health Care Consulting

After a 20-plus-year run of explosive growth, the consulting industry experienced a rude awakening in the early 2000s, when the world's largest corporations—consulting's most significant clients—suddenly retreated into cost-cutting mode. Over a two-year period, consulting firms literally went from feast to famine, as their primary clients turned off the tap on new projects and external consulting engagements. In the intervening years, the industry as a whole has been trying to rebuild itself.

Even during those trying times, though, the health care segment of the consulting market performed exceptionally well. In 2002 (when industry-wide revenues stayed flat), health care consulting revenues actually posted modest growth. And, according to Kennedy Information, this trend is likely to continue over the next several years, as revenue growth in the health care consulting segment is expected to outpace growth in most other consulting sectors.

Unlike other industries, the health care sector itself is relatively impervious to fluctuations in the economic cycle. No matter how the economy is doing, there is always demand for health care products and services, and, likewise, for consultants who can help their clients offer these products and services more efficiently. Since demand for health care consulting services isn't as vulnerable when the economy wanes, it's growing faster than any other consulting segment—which makes it an attractive specialty for both consulting firms and job seekers.

For simplicity's sake, diversified consulting firms typically classify health care consulting as one of their *industry* specialties. Strictly speaking, however, health care isn't really an industry. It refers to a combination of large, private-sector suppliers and organizations—such as pharmaceutical, biotechnology, and medical device companies—as well as regional health provider systems and government entities. Depending on the breadth and depth of their expertise, health care consultants may advise the following types of organizations:

- Life sciences: pharmaceuticals, biotechnology, medical devices

- Providers: hospitals, integrated delivery networks (IDNs, which deliver coordinated services via multiple sites), academic medical centers (AMCs), physician organizations, outpatient centers, clinics, non-U.S. national health systems

- Insurers and payers: Blue Cross/Blue Shield organizations, other insurance organizations, regional and national health maintenance organizations (HMOs), national health insurers outside the United States

- Government and associated entities: Department of Defense; Department of Health and Human Services; Department of Veteran Affairs; city, state, and national health care organizations

- Health organizations: facilities planning, health policy, nonprofit organizations

Health care consulting practices—whether they are small specialized boutique consultancies or industry groups within larger consulting firms—may offer expertise in all of these segments or they may offer advisory services in only one or two areas. As you prepare for your interviews, you should make note of which types of health care consulting each potential employer offers. For example, Booz Allen Hamilton is the leading consulting practice to government health organizations, while McKinsey primarily advises pharmaceutical firms and medical products companies. Each of these firms offers some sort of health care expertise, but that means a slightly different thing at each company.

THE PLAYERS

Though this sector is dominated by larger players, smaller specialty consultancies—many with fewer than 100 or 200 consultants—have also made a dent in the health care consulting market. As one expert says, "The health care consulting marketplace, like the overall health care industry itself, is a heterogeneous arena of hundreds of specialty firms. Many of these firms fly under the radar of their larger consulting firm rivals." As a result, smaller firms can (and often do) compete for business with larger firms, offering depth in industry expertise, while their counterparts at larger strategy firms argue that their experience across multiple industries gives them a distinct advantage.

Sample of Top Health Care Consulting Practices

Firm	Website
Abt Associates	www.abtassociates.com
Accenture	www.accenture.com
ACS Healthcare Solutions	www.acs-hcs.com
Aon Consulting	www.aon.com
Bain & Co.	www.bain.com
Battelle	www.battelle.org
BearingPoint	www.bearingpoint.com
Booz Allen Hamilton	www.boozallen.com
Boston Consulting Group	www.bcg.com
Capgemini	www.capgemini.com
Cardinal Health Consulting Services	www.cardinal.com/mps/servicesolution/consult/home.asp
Computer Sciences Corporation	www.csc.com
Deloitte Consulting	www.deloitte.com
Easton Associates	www.eastonassociates.com
GE Healthcare	www.gehealthcare.com
Huron Consulting Group	www.huronconsultinggroup.com
IBM Business Consulting Services	www.ibm.com/services
Kurt Salmon Associates	www.kurtsalmon.com
McKinsey & Company	www.mckinsey.com
Navigant Consulting	www.navigantconsulting.com
PA Consulting Group	www.paconsulting.com
PAREXEL Consulting	www.parexel.com
PricewaterhouseCoopers Health Advisory Services	www.pwc.com
Quintiles Consulting/The Lewin Group	www.quintiles.com/quintilesconsulting.com
Stockamp and Associates	www.stockamp.com
Unisys	www.unisys.com
Wellspring Partners	www.wp-ltd.com

Source: *The Healthcare Consulting Marketplace, Kennedy Information*, Inc., 2005; WetFeet analysis

OUTLOOK

The health care consulting market has seen stronger growth than most other consulting specialties in the first half of the first decade of the new millennium. According to The Healthcare Consulting Marketplace, a 2005 report by Kennedy Information, by 2008 it will be the second-largest consulting sector, with growth driven by key market segments like life sciences, providers, insurers/payers, and government.

Opportunities within the life sciences segment include helping pharmaceutical companies rein in costs, expand into businesses other than prescription drugs, and deal with financial issues as VC funding of pharmaceutical and biotech companies increases. In the health care providers' segment, organizations that are going global, dealing with talent shortages (such as the shortage of nurses), and striving to control costs are key growth areas for consulting.

" Health care consulting is an exciting place to be because the industry is undergoing a lot of change very quickly. Because of all of the public policy issues, regulatory issues, and insurance issues, the engagements tend to be so complex.

In the insurers and payers segment, up-and-coming issues include the move toward customer-directed health care in the form of Health Spending Accounts (HSAs); the increase in "personalized" and "orphan" drugs ("Personalized" drugs are fine-tuned for specific patient populations, e.g. BiDil, a heart medication for African Americans; "orphan" drugs are drugs for rare diseases); and the move toward a "pay-for-performance" model for compensating health care professionals. In the government segment, areas of opportunity include the crisis in vaccine supply and development and increasing demand for health care consulting help from non-U.S. governments.

THE WORK

Because health care consultants work for clients in a variety of sectors, the engagements in which they're involved are equally diverse. The type of work that you'll do as a health care consultant depends largely on which subset of the industry your client represents, whether it's a life sciences company, provider, insurer, payer, or government agency. One insider describes the fundamental differences among the types of projects on which he's worked: "Pharmaceutical companies are run much more like a business, so you're often dealing with issues that you'd deal with in any other business: product positioning, effective marketing, distribution channels, and so forth. On the other hand, provider organizations—such as hospitals—are primarily trying to react to what's going on around them. So even though both of these clients fall under the health care umbrella, the types of engagements and the work that we do will be completely different."

Regardless of the health care segment that you're advising, you'll likely confront some of the most intellectually challenging, analytically rigorous, and potentially rewarding assignments that the consulting profession has to offer. "Health care consulting is an exciting place to be because the industry is undergoing a lot of change very quickly," says one insider. "Because of all the public policy issues, regulatory issues, and insurance issues, the engagements tend to be so complex. In that way, I think that it's much more interesting to work in health care consulting than it would be to do consulting in a more stagnant industry. It requires more intelligent thinking than other types of work. On the flip side, though, it can be frustrating; a lot of grand ideas never get implemented."

Engagements can be classified by the type of client (pharmaceutical, provider, etc.) and even further by the type of consulting service that's provided (strategy, operations, IT, or HR consulting).

CASE STUDIES

The case studies here represent a cross section of the types of projects that you might work on as a health care consultant.

Provider Workforce-Management Study

One of the five busiest U.S. trauma centers was unable to fill permanent positions or replace its traveling medical professionals with full-time staff due to its noncompetitive rates and high per-employee caseload. The facility retained a health care consulting firm to strengthen its attractiveness to candidates and elevate its presence, both regionally and nationally. By documenting that competitors were paying core staff above published rates, the consulting firm convinced the client to effectively increase its union-managed wage scale. The consulting firms also executed a far-reaching recruitment plan to boost the volume of qualified candidates.

Pharmaceutical Strategy Study

An international pharmaceutical company was falling short of its goal to bring two and a half blockbuster NCEs (new chemical entities) to market each year. The company had an extensive research and development (R&D) project portfolio, but its R&D process was cumbersome; it lacked appropriate prioritization and clear cut-off criteria. As a result, the R&D organization was scattered and lacked cross-functional project management. The company needed a new R&D strategy to lower costs while increasing the output of new products, so it retained a leading consulting firm to redefine its strategy to maximize the value of its investments. As a result, the company decided to focus resources on just 6 of its 11 therapeutic areas and reduce its R&D budget by 4 percent of sales over a five-year period. Implementing this new R&D strategy allowed the company to increase investments in therapeutic areas of focus and substantially improve operations.

Medical Devices Operations Study

The client—a $40-million producer of medical devices and tests used in hospitals—recorded revenue and profits significantly below its expectations. The company's factory was running out of capacity, requiring major investment and significant disruption to the business. The client engaged a top-tier consulting firm to evaluate its manufacturing strategy and recommend changes. The consulting firm analyzed the company's plant capacity, technology platforms, and outsourcing opportunities. Its recommendations were reviewed with the company's board of directors at a two-day offsite meeting and were approved for immediate action. By increasing capacity in the existing plant, the company was able to avoid a costly new expansion plan and boost production significantly.

Provider Operations Study

A prominent West Coast health system (which included a very large hospital and hundreds of academic faculty) was experiencing a sustained period of poor performance and declining collections in its professional-fee business office. Communication between the professional billing operation and the health system's various patient-care services departments was poor. The health system engaged a consulting firm to lead a process improvement project for the entire professional fee-billing operation—from the initial point-of-patient registration to the final point-of-account balance collection. Based on the consulting firm's recommendations, the organization was able to increase its total collection rate on an ongoing basis by more than 15 percent.

GETTING HIRED

At the larger strategy consulting firms, such as McKinsey, the Boston Consulting Group, Bain, and Booz Allen, recent graduates join the firm as generalists and not as dedicated consultants for any particular practice area. During the first two years of their tenure, business analysts (or associates, depending on the nomenclature of the firm) may work with case teams tackling issues in any number of industries. The likelihood of working on a health care project depends—at least in part—on the staffing needs and the location of the office in which you work. If you're hired into the Philadelphia office, for example, you're perhaps more likely to work with a pharmaceutical client than you would if you worked in Los Angeles, due to the higher geographic concentration of pharmaceutical companies in the Mid-Atlantic region.

As consultants become more senior, they're exposed to more opportunities to specialize in a given industry or function. One insider at a strategy firm explains that, "for the first two to four years, you're definitely a generalist. You don't really specialize. But as you become more senior, you can begin to carve out a specialization for yourself. If your interest is health care, you'd express an interest in that practice area, and the firm would make an effort to staff you on those types of projects." For the most part, the same is true at the larger consulting firms that launch formal, on-campus recruiting processes, including Accenture, Deloitte, and IBM.

If you've got your sights set on a smaller consulting firm that specializes in health care, it will be substantially more difficult to get hired directly out of an undergraduate program without directly relevant industry experience. Because these firms are relatively small (sometimes as few as 20 consultants), they typically don't conduct formal on-campus recruiting efforts. Instead, they hire on a just-in-time basis and generally require candidates to demonstrate prior industry experience in health care, an advanced degree (often multiple advanced degrees) and (often) consulting experience with another firm. As a general rule, the smaller and more specialized the consulting firm, the less likely it is that you'll be hired either as an undergraduate, or as an experienced hire without a track record of success in both health care and consulting. With such small practices and lean project teams, these firms don't have the critical mass to offer extensive formal training programs for new hires. Industry and functional expertise counts a lot, so it's considerably easier to join as an experienced lateral hire than as a recent college graduate or newly minted MBA.

Human Resources Consulting

If you've already done a fair bit of research on consulting (and certainly if you've attended an on-campus company presentation by a consulting firm), you've probably heard these companies claim that their greatest asset is their people. In fact, hearing a company trumpet this sentiment is a little bit like hearing that four out of five dentists prefer a particular brand of toothpaste; it doesn't mean all that much anymore, primarily because the concept has been overused in marketing efforts (and because the fifth dentist could never agree with the rest of the group). Even though the "greatest asset is our people" shtick is ubiquitous, there's a lot of truth to the sentiment underneath all the marketing hype. The notion isn't unique to consulting firms and other expertise-intensive businesses, either; virtually *any* type of company can legitimately claim that its greatest asset is its people. On the average, 60 to 70 percent of a company's expenditures are related to human capital: the cost of recruiting, hiring, training, developing, and retaining top people to keep an organization competitive.

Human resources consultants (or human capital consultants, as they are called at many firms) help their clients make the most of these people-related investments. They help organizations understand, develop, implement, and quantify their HR programs and policies. The service for which these firms are perhaps best known is providing advice on compensation and benefits. "When you say HR consulting, most people think of compensation and benefits. These are the most revenue-producing areas of HR consulting firms," says an insider. This trend is largely driven by employers' need to recruit and retain employees and to motivate them to higher levels of performance; especially in a tight labor market, the costs of recruiting but not retaining productive employees are substantial, so companies want to ensure that their compensation and benefits packages are both attractive and competitive.

Projects in this consulting segment aren't limited to compensation and benefits services, however. Over the past two decades, the human resources function has gradually morphed from a largely administrative department to a more strategically oriented one. To a greater extent than ever, HR departments actively participate in the development and achievement of companies' organizational goals, and HR consultants tackle more strategic issues related to leveraging the collective skills and capabilities of clients' employees.

Though the work of many HR professionals—including HR consultants—reflects this increasingly strategic orientation, HR-process outsourcing is still the bread and butter of many an HR consulting firm. A recent study conducted by the Society of Human Resource Professionals (SHRP) and the Bureau of National Affairs (BNA) reveals that 75 percent of organizations outsource one or more functions traditionally performed by an internal HR department. For many organizations, HR process outsourcing doesn't simply represent a cost-cutting measure—instead, it represents a way for companies to focus on their core businesses and redirect their own HR professionals from administrative to strategic tasks.

THE PLAYERS

The HR consulting sector is dominated by large consulting firms. Most of the major consulting firms offer service lines related to HR, but true to the consulting profession, they give them fancier names, such as "Human Performance" (at Accenture), "Organization" (at The Boston Consulting Group), and "Organizations, People & Performance" (at Booz Allen Hamilton). Among consultancies dedicated to HR, a few large firms dominate the field: Mercer HR Consulting, Hewitt Associates, Watson Wyatt, and Towers Perrin are considered the "Big Four" of this segment. In addition, more specialized, boutique firms offer services that can handle virtually any HR issue.

To further complicate the competitive landscape for HR consultancies, leaders of non-HR firms are making a play for services traditionally provided by the HR specialists. In particular, firms such as IBM, EDS, and CSC are dipping into the HR outsourcing market, which represents a sizeable business opportunity for both new and established players.

Sample of Top HR Consulting Practices

Firm	Website
Accenture	www.accenture.com
ACS	www.acs-inc.com
ADP	www.adp.com
Aon Consulting	www.aon.com
ARINSO	www.arinso.com
Black Mountain Group	www.blackmountaingroup.com
Ceridian	www.ceridian.com
CitiStreet	www.citistreetonline.com
CSC	www.csc.com
Curcio Webb	www.curciowebb.com
Deloitte – Human Capital	www.deloitte.com
Development Dimensions International	www.ddiworld.com
EquaTerra	www.equaterra.com
Ernst & Young	www.ey.com
Everest Group	www.everestgrp.com
Fidelity	www.fidelity.com
Hay Group	www.haygroup.com
Hewitt Associates	www.hewitt.com
IBM Global Services	www.ibm.com/services
LogicaCMG	www.logicacmg.com
Manpower	www.manpower.com
Mercer Human Resource Consulting	www.mercerhr.com
Merrill Lynch	www.ml.com
Milliman Global	www.milliman.com
Morneau Sobeco	www.morneausobeco.com
PricewaterhouseCoopers	www.pwc.com
Right Management Consultants	www.right.com
Russell Investment Group	www.russell.com
SAP	www.sap.com

Firm	Website
The Segal Company	www.segalco.com
Towers Perrin	www.towersperrin.com
TPI	www.tpi.net
Watson Wyatt Worldwide	www.watsonwyatt.com
Xchanging	www.xchanging.com

Source: *The Healthcare Consulting Marketplace*, Kennedy Information, Inc., 2005; Hoovers.com; WetFeet analysis

OUTLOOK

According to The HR Consulting and Outsourcing Markets, a 2005 report by Kennedy Information, the HR consulting market—a $13.3 billion market at the time of the report—should grow to become a nearly $15.5 billion market by 2008.

There are several factors that are facilitating growth in this sector. One is merger and acquisition activity: Industry consolidation means more work for HR consultants. Another is executive compensation: Such issues as shifting away from using stock options as a major part of executive compensation are driving growth in this area. Another hot area, a symptom of out-of-control cost increases in U.S. health care, is providing advice to corporations on their health insurance benefits. Other areas projected to drive growth in HR consulting include advising companies on how to deal with the shortage of highly skilled talent, how to enhance HR effectiveness while reducing HR costs, and how to go about outsourcing HR functions.

Factors constraining growth include limited corporate HR budgets, reluctance on the part of corporations to invest in talent development, to change retirement plan strategies due to changing government regulations and accounting standards, and to invest in HR technology, and downward pressure on consulting rates, especially in the benefits-consulting arena.

HR outsourcing is big business, and getting bigger by the year. Indeed, it was already a $32.7 billion business by the time the 2005 Kennedy Information report ("The HR Consulting and Outsourcing Markets") was published—that's about two and a half times the size of the market for HR consulting—and Kennedy Information projects that this sector will grow at an annual rate of 25 percent through 2008. We're likely to see significant consolidation in this sector, as companies endeavor to lower costs via achieving greater economies of scale.

Longer-term, the general outlook for HR consulting and outsourcing is good. According to recent reports from the U.S. Census Bureau, the Government Accountability Office (formerly the General Accounting Office), the National Bureau of Economic Research, and the Conference Board (among others), the retirement of baby boomers in the next few years will translate into a major shortage of labor as early as 2010—meaning there will continue to be HR issues that companies look to experts in the field to help them deal with. Regardless of whether the labor shortage is demographic fact or fiction born of wishful thinking—consulting for HR is and will remain a huge business. After all, organizations ultimately rely on people for their success; as long as companies must hire, fire, train, pay, promote, and motivate employees, they will face complex people issues that can have a substantial impact on their bottom line. Given that this is the case, HR consultants will be able to make a compelling business case for their services for the foreseeable future, labor shortage or not.

If you're thinking of a career in HR consulting, be sure that you're comfortable with the consulting part of the equation: the nature of the work, the distinct consulting culture, and the work/life balance challenges that are unavoidable. "It deals with HR topics, but fundamentally it's a consulting firm," says an insider. "It's the more touchy-feely of the consulting tracks. If you like the variety and challenge of consulting, but also want to feel like your job makes a difference in the lives of people, I think HR [consulting] comes closer to that than strategy [consulting]."

Even so, the work is often strategic, focusing on the issues of running a large company. A lot of it is data-driven, too, as it is in actuarial consulting, which involves financial planning based on the company's long-term hiring projections. "The whole consulting culture is present," says an insider. "It's a lot of analysis of papers and programs. The culture is very performance-oriented. You work very hard." However, don't expect the name recognition in HR consulting that you'd expect at other big consulting firms. "No one knows you, unless they know about the business," says an insider. Still, HR consulting firms often enjoy a fairly impressive roster of Fortune 500 clients. According to one insider, "Even though not everyone knows what my company does, our clients are usually household names. Our clients are definitely companies that your grand-mother has heard of."

SAMPLE CASE STUDIES

HR consulting engagements are as varied as the HR function itself. Projects in this segment are hardly limited to compensation and benefits services. The projects that our insiders describe involve everything from helping a company reorganize and cultivate a culture after a merger to developing leadership training programs to managing employee communications. Other HR consultants might help an organization establish its corporate values, review another's performance management system, or design job roles and job descriptions for a company with a rapidly expanding workforce. Two other areas of HR consulting are eHR (or HRe), which is focused on bringing all HR transactions online—everything from performance management and career planning systems to training—and HR information systems (HRIS). The case studies below represent a cross section of the types of engagements in which HR consultants are likely to be involved.

Change Management Study

The client, a Fortune 500 manufacturing company, wanted to trim jobs and expenses without a significant negative impact on the organization's people, human resources function, and culture. The company retained a top-tier consulting firm to conduct workforce transition strategies including workforce assessment, severance management, talent management, legal compliance review, and communications strategies. In addition, it reduced costs associated with health and prescription plans, ultimately enabling the employer to provide a wider range of employee benefits at a reduced cost to the client. As a result, operating expenses were scaled back on several fronts, allowing the client to focus on the marketplace and future business opportunities. Employee morale improved as employees embraced the new benefit programs and individuals were able to better align their goals and objectives with the strategic vision of the organization.

Retirement Services Study

Like many firms in the last few years, a global transportation company's retirement plan assets were challenged by a decline in the equities markets. The company hired a leading HR consulting firm to reengineer its retirement program—including its administration—to make its delivery of services to key stakeholders more effective and efficient. After examining the existing structure of the retirement function, the consulting firm designed a new streamlined structure for the team, specifying new responsibilities and processes for the function to undertake. Finally, the consulting team highlighted key retirement administration activities that needed additional focus from the organization, including compliance, management reporting, and strategic support to units and leadership. As a result, the company has a new centralized, consolidated, and streamlined retirement function that provides enhanced human capital and subject matter expertise to business unit leaders. Outsourcing the administration of the retirement plans has resulted in additional efficiencies and service improvements. And with the retirement team now managing these relationships, the company will achieve maximum value from these investments.

HRIS Study

A global defense company with 100,000 employees wanted to align executive performance with business results by creating a single source for up-to-date personal information on executive compensation, financial performance, and bonus metrics. The company felt that only a custom-built Web application could provide the integrated online resource that would meet its needs. If developed and hosted internally, the site would challenge HR, IT, communication, and other internal personnel by adding programming, data integration, ongoing content updates, and technical maintenance to their duties. Instead of building a custom site, the company implemented one of the existing, off-the-shelf online tools developed by a leading consulting firm. This solution provided more than 90 percent of the functionality required by the company at half the cost of a custom solution. The site was easily tailored to the company's specifications, and now provides executives with a quickly accessed, clear understanding of personal financial opportunity.

GETTING HIRED

While a few of these firms (including Hewitt and Mercer HR) conduct recruiting processes on campuses nationwide, many others do not, relying instead on their online job application processes to source and screen qualified candidates. The firms that do recruit at undergraduate campuses typically focus on two distinct roles: the actuarial consultant position and the business analyst role within the firm's outsourcing practice. Actuarial consultant positions (not surprisingly) require a bachelor's degree in actuarial science, mathematics, or business. On the benefits delivery side, firms may recruit business analysts (who have typically majored in a business discipline such as finance or management or have an engineering background), business systems analysts (who generally hold degrees in management information systems, computer science, or systems engineering), and programmer analysts (whose roles are the most technical, requiring a related major and prior programming experience).

For their more strategic HR consulting work, firms usually seek lateral hires (rather than new graduates) who bring functional expertise. For these types of positions, an MBA is universally considered a plus, but relevant industry or functional expertise is perhaps the single most important prerequisite. HR consulting firms typically do not launch extensive recruiting efforts on business school campuses, with occasional exceptions. The best way to pursue opportunities in these firms' strategic consulting practices is to keep apprised of openings through the firm's website, and (as always) to network with people who work for the companies in which you're most interested.

Beyond the HR specialist firms, the larger, diversified consultancies with dedicated HR practices (such as IBM Global Services, Accenture, or Deloitte) offer ample opportunities to join the firm as generalists with the option of developing an area of expertise after a few years on the job. Firms like these *do* conduct extensive on-campus recruiting efforts for undergraduates, MBAs, and other advanced-degree candidates. Though you probably won't be able to specialize in HR consulting within the first few years of your career, the client exposure and on-the-job training can often lay the groundwork for specializing down the line, whether you decide to stay with the same firm or migrate to a company that specializes in HR consulting.

Information Technology/ Systems Consulting

If you're technically inclined and love designing computer systems and applications—and you're not allergic to acronyms—this may be the area for you. Information technology (IT) consultants find ways to apply technology to achieve a client's business goals, typically taking on large projects to design, implement, and manage their clients' information and computer systems. To do this, they either work with a company's information systems department or its senior financial or operating officers.

Even though a weakened economy dampened demand for consulting services in the early part of the decade, this segment of the industry continues to generate a substantial portion of the consulting market's overall revenue. According to recent research by experts at Harvard Business School, more than 50 percent of today's capital budgeting expenditures involve computing in one form or another. As a result, IT and systems consulting revenues account for a much bigger part of the overall market than strategy consulting—60 to 70 percent of the overall consulting market, according to Plunkett Research.

Information technology could reasonably be classified as an operations issue—computer systems are one tool a manager uses to operate a company. Indeed, technology has become an integral component of a comprehensive operations strategy; today, a company's entire supply chain—not just its customer relationships—is often managed electronically. But unlike other business processes, IT has the capability to *create* business strategy, not just support it. In fact, the strategic implications of IT are so far-reaching that literally *all* consulting firms—regardless of their official classification in the consulting taxonomy—have had to develop and integrate IT expertise into their existing practices. They must provide strategic perspectives along with implementation savvy. If companies cannot realize the strategic competitive advantages of IT because of failure to address implementation challenges, they face considerable risks to the long-term sustainability of their business.

THE PLAYERS

Larger firms dominate the IT consulting landscape, with the biggest firms, like IBM and Accenture, dwarfing most of the competition. Still, a recent study conducted by the ITSMA (an IT market research firm) suggests that there's still plenty of opportunity for smaller, niche-focused boutique firms. Indeed, there are hundreds, if not thousands, of small IT-focused consulting firms across the country, meeting niche IT needs as well as the needs of smaller businesses.

Perhaps the most influential trend to shape the competitive IT consulting market landscape has been the emergence of computer software and hardware producers in the consulting business. Experts suggest that the seeds for this trend were planted back in the 1990s; as IT consulting revenue skyrocketed, software manufacturing companies watched their profit margins shrink as global competition intensified and their products became commoditized. Adding consulting services to their offerings gives these firms the opportunity to build stable repeat revenue on top of their manufacturing bases, and they have a built-in clientele of existing customers and end users.

Leading the charge of product manufacturers into IT consulting is none other than Big Blue. IBM's consulting and outsourcing services account for more than half of its $91 billion in annual revenue. Other firms, such as SAP and Hewlett Packard, have developed specialized consulting services to sell along with their signature software packages. In fact, virtually all of the major hardware and software companies—HP, Sun, Oracle, and Dell—have their eyes on increased service revenues through consulting and outsourcing, either through wholly owned subsidiaries or partnerships with consulting firms.

Sample of Top IT Consulting Practices

Firm	Website
Accenture	www.accenture.com
Atos Origin	www.atosorigin.com
BearingPoint	www.bearingpoint.com
Capgemini	www.capgemini.com
Cognizant Technology Solutions	www.cognizant.com
CGI Group	www.cgi.com
CSC	www.csc.com
Deloitte	www.deloitte.com
DiamondCluster International	www.diamondcluster.com
EDS	www.eds.com
Fujitsu	www.fujitsu.com
Gartner	www.gartner.com
Hewlett-Packard	www.hp.com
IBM Business Consulting Services	www.ibm.com/services
Lockheed Martin	www.lockheedmartin.com
LogicaCMG	www.logicacmg.com
Oracle Corporation	www.oracle.com
PA Consulting Group	www.paconsulting.com
SAP	www.sap.com
Science Applications International Corporation	www.saic.com
Siemens Business Services	www.sbs.usa.siemens.com
Tata Consultancy Services	www.tcs.com
Unisys	www.unisys.com
Wipro Technologies	www.wipro.com

Source: *The Systems Integration Marketplace*, Kennedy Information, Inc., 2004; IT Strategy and Planning, Kennedy Information, Inc., 2004; *IT Consulting & Systems Integration Leaders*, Kennedy Information, Inc., 2005; Hoovers.com; WetFeet analysis

OUTLOOK

During the 1990s, technology consulting was red-hot. Companies of all stripes spent money as if it grew on trees to purchase new computer hardware and software, to have that new technology implemented and integrated with their existing systems, and to learn how to maximize the benefit they got from their technology purchases. With stock prices on the rise and VCs writing ever-larger checks, companies faced little in the way of cost constraints. Factor in the Y2K scare and companies' fear of falling behind their competitors in technology, and we saw rivers of money flowing freely to consultancies that sold, implemented, and/or advised companies about technology.

Then came the bust. Funding sources dried up, and companies that had recently ruled the world were suddenly struggling to survive—those that hadn't gone out of business, that is. And, of course, spending on technology implementation and consulting dropped precipitously, leading to layoffs of tech consultants at firms big and small.

These days, companies are still relatively conservative about IT expenditures; it will probably be a long time until corporate America is willing to spend on IT as freely as it did during the boom. That hurts IT consultants, of course. So does reduced demand and lower prices for new technology and technology implementation services due to the rise of the BPO market. But the darkest days seem to be over. Observers say that corporate spending, while more selective than it was back in the go-go '90s, is on the rise. And tech hiring is also strengthening. According to a recent CNNMoney.com article, "Demand for technology workers in the United States continues to grow in spite of American companies shifting more technology work overseas" ("Study Says U.S. Tech Hiring Grows," CNNMoney.com, 2/23/06). In a recent survey, Silicon Valley executives expressed "cautious optimism" about employment in 2006 and beyond, with 56 percent reporting that they plan to increase their companies' workforces in 2006, compared to just 8 percent planning to cut jobs ("Silicon Valley Job Outlook Improving," *San Francisco Chronicle*, 2/17/06). Increased demand for technology, of course, means increased demand for technology consultants who help companies figure out their technology strategy and then decide what technologies they should purchase—and possibly help implement them and train employees in their use, as well..

The real story in technology consulting, though, is outsourcing. This is where companies hire other companies, usually located in parts of the world where labor is cheaper, to handle entire chunks of their IT and business process needs. Indeed, BPO is a $300 billion market, and is expected to grow at a rate of nearly 12 percent annually between 2005 and 2009 ("Consulting Around BPO and Transformation," Kennedy Information). There will be a corresponding increase in the need for consulting services to help corporate clients make outsourcing decisions, and then manage their outsourcing efforts.

THE WORK

IT consulting engagements can be seen from a few different perspectives. Engagements are often described in terms of five broad categories, which roughly correspond to the chronological order in which companies address a technological need or opportunity:

1. Devising an IT *strategy* that will facilitate the company's broader business plan

2. Managing the *design* of a specific technology solution that will support this strategy

3. Overseeing the *implementation* of the new system

4. Providing *integration* services to make disparate systems compatible

5. Assuming ongoing *management* responsibilities for all or part of a client's IT operations

Though the strategy consulting firms (like Bain, BCG, and McKinsey) maintain IT consulting services, they tend to focus on the earlier stages of the process; they offer expertise in aligning business strategy with IT strategy, and advise their clients on the organization-wide process and behavior changes they can expect as a result of the IT implementation. As clients progress toward later steps, their consultants typically need less general business knowledge and more industry and technical knowledge.

In addition, IT consulting firms may specialize in one type of IT strategy (for instance, e-business), a particular application (for example, customer relationship management solutions), a particular component of the client's infrastructure (such as supply chain management), or a specific software package that it can help the client customize and implement. An IT consulting firm (or an IT consulting practice within a larger services firm) may offer services in any of these areas.

Industry insiders suggest that consulting engagements involving large-scale implementations of enterprise software are less plentiful than they were a few years back. Newcomers to IT consulting should expect to see computer-to-computer communications driving the IT consulting industry forward over the next few years, much as the Internet, e-commerce, and Y2K propelled the industry in the IT consulting days of yesteryear. Computer-to-computer communication effectively accelerates the pace of business, and it is changing the way companies respond to shifts in customer demand for their goods and services. "There's a huge wealth of information in point-of-sale data that the company can leverage to its benefit—not just about the customer, but about the ways in which the organization can improve its supply chain and enhance its bottom line," explains one industry insider. "It's that type of analysis that's driving the industry right now." Consulting firms that help clients capture this wealth of data will be well positioned to succeed in this competitive landscape.

CASE STUDIES

The following case studies represent a cross section of the strategic and operational issues that IT consultants typically face:

IT Strategy Case Study

A national specialty retailer of better women's apparel, shoes, and accessories lacked an integrated system to support product development and production. Its product tracking and decision-making information was housed across multiple software packages, custom applications, and standardized spreadsheets that were manually updated and exchanged among functions and offices. Simple questions—such as the number of units at a particular factory—could not be answered without extensive manual effort. A leading IT consulting firm performed a comprehensive assessment of current systems and processes and provided a series of recommendations to strategically position the organization for future growth. System recommendations included an assessment of potential vendors, an outline of the services provided by each of those vendors, cost and time estimates, and a detailed project plan. The client expects that operational improvements supported by the new, integrated systems will reduce administrative costs almost 50 percent, while reducing both operating risk and cycle time.

E-Commerce Study

The client—the direct marketing division of a leading global retailer—was facing rapid growth and expansion into e-commerce. The division realized that its existing technology and processes would not support this future business; the company needed to select, test, implement, and integrate new facilities, business and warehousing systems, and processes. The client selected an IT consulting firm to design new facilities with new procedures and technology applications. Developing new business systems—and integrating them with existing warehouse management systems—was crucial to the client's transition to new operations, so the consulting firm worked closely with client personnel to ensure that integration was seamless. Collectively, the client and the consulting firm implemented and integrated the system very quickly, enabling the company to ship holiday orders on time and compete at industry-leading service levels.

Customer Relationship Management Study

The client—a major U.S. bank that provides credit card, banking, and financial services to ten million customers—wanted to introduce an information distribution and delivery infrastructure that would enhance its competitive position in the financial services industry. To achieve this goal, they needed to strengthen customer ties weakened by a decade of consolidation and cost-cutting. In addition, they needed to consolidate the customer data that was currently housed in more than 33 nonintegrated systems. With the help of a leading consulting firm, the client implemented a customer relationship management (CRM) solution that would help it cultivate and nurture personalized customer relationships. The CRM system provided a central information repository, allowing the company to identify its most valuable customers, understand and analyze customer behavior, develop the optimum mix of products and services, and tailor marketing campaigns to address customer needs. Furthermore, this personalized approach allowed the bank to provide relevant, timely information to customers, thereby increasing its share of each customer's business.

Supply Chain Management Case Study

One of the largest specialty chemical companies in the world wanted to integrate its suppliers and customers using Internet-based technology. To achieve this goal, the company engaged a top-tier consulting firm to develop a strategy for optimizing the demand for its construction chemical business. First, the consulting firm conducted a preliminary strategy assessment and vendor selection process. Next, it provided a long-term strategic plan for optimizing demand chain management, and—based on this plan— helped the client implement a solution that was easily integrated with its existing information systems. By rapidly deploying its supply chain management, the consulting firm helped its client increase revenue, reduce costs, improve customer retention, and enhance its competitive advantage. The channel now provides customers with real-time product pricing and information, 24/7 order entry and tracking, and just-in-time deliverables.

GETTING HIRED

In general, IT consulting requires large teams of people who actually do the computer work, rather than simply give advice on a particular IT strategy or approach. As a result, there are usually more opportunities for people from undergraduate or technical backgrounds than from MBA programs. Hiring criteria are refreshingly transparent; rather than navigating a series of brainteasers and market-sizing questions, candidates for IT jobs—whether they're entry-level candidates or experienced hires—must prove first and foremost that they have the technical expertise necessary to perform the responsibilities of the job.

Undergraduates with degrees in computer science, computer engineering, computer information systems, electrical engineering, mechanical engineering, human factors engineering, chemical engineering, and materials science are in high demand to fill entry-level IT consulting positions. IT consulting firms also consider candidates who have studied other disciplines such as math, finance, business, and marketing. Some IT consulting practices (especially firms that hire large numbers of entry-level staff each year, such as Accenture) hire for these positions through on-campus recruiting processes. Others rely on their online recruiting systems to target and select qualified applicants.

Aside from the required technical aptitude, the skills required of IT consultants and their counterparts in strategy consulting are actually quite similar: Problem-solving skills, interpersonal aptitude, teamwork, intellectual curiosity, a customer-service orientation, and communication skills are top priorities for recruiters in this area. Strong analytical skills and a passion for improving business processes for client companies also help. "The way I see it, we're helping corporate America make the best possible use of its human capital. It's that side of the business—the interplay between technology and human capital—that I find fascinating about work in IT consulting. We don't just sit in front of computers all day doing coding or working on systems implementation." Credibility, good judgment, and poise are also essential. "From day one, you're put in front of the client as an expert. If the recruiter that interviews you can't see putting you in that position, you're not going to get the job, regardless of your technical expertise."

Picking and Choosing

As you've probably concluded by now, there are numerous yellow brick roads leading to the Emerald City in the world of consulting (and quite a few different Emerald Cities, for that matter). How do you go about choosing the one that's right for you? Chances are that if you're reading this guide, you're not necessarily considering and comparing all three types of consulting: health care, HR, and IT. More likely, you fall into one of three camps:

1. You've read all about management consulting in our WetFeet Insider Guide to *Careers in Management Consulting* and the work sounds interesting, but you're curious to know what other types of consulting may be a good fit for you.

2. You're considering careers in consulting along with their counterparts in private industry: comparing a job in HR consulting with a career in the HR department of a company, for example, or considering both IT consulting and technology firms.

3. You may already have decided on your calling, but want to know the best avenue to pursue. If your passion is health care consulting, for example, should you try to get a job with a strategy firm, or should you conduct a more targeted job search toward consulting firms that specialize in serving health care clients?

We'll walk through each of these situations and let you know what factors you should consider in each case.

THINKING ABOUT CONSULTING?

If you've read our other consulting guides and like the idea of advising companies on critical issues—and you have an interest in and aptitude for IT, then we don't have to tell you that IT consulting may be a logical place to look. The most important thing to remember if you fall into this category (regardless of whether your interests and experiences lie in IT, HR, or health care) is that *you fundamentally have to like the idea of being a consultant.* Though the perks and the challenges inherent to the job may be slightly different from specialty to specialty, many of the themes that we explored in our strategy consulting guide are relevant here. If you've read another of our consulting guides and are interested in the profession but intimidated by the work or the interviewing process, think long and hard about pursuing a career in an operations or industry consulting role. There's a reason this guide isn't called *Consulting Lite.*

What Insiders (and Outsiders) Say

People go into consulting for lots of reasons. After extensive industry research and interviews with a number of people who have gone into consulting, as well as those who have decided not to, our impression is that consulting is a great career for a few people, a good short-term job for some, and a bad place for many others.

Best Reasons for Going into Consulting

- It's a great way to learn about lots of industries and functions without committing to any one of them for life.

- The opportunity to work with lots of bright, motivated, and social colleagues, thanks to the industry-wide focus on recruiting high achievers and "*people* people"

- Good pay, benefits, and perks

- It may give you a chance to see the world, even if that world is sometimes Pittsburgh. (Pittsburgh is actually pretty cool.)

- If you change your mind and switch to another firm (or another profession, for that matter) after a few years, there's no stigma attached: Moving around is par for the course for most consultants.

- Telling CEOs what to do gives your ego a great massage.

- A belief that consultants make business—and the world—a better place.

- Variety—no matter what consulting specialty you choose, virtually no two engagements are ever the same.

- Considering making a transition into a specific industry (e.g., health care) or a specific function (e.g., HR or IT) in corporate America? Your experience tackling a range of issues unique to that specialty will make you a compelling candidate.

- You'll accrue a strong contact network will help you throughout your career.

Best Reasons for Not Going into Consulting

- You have a conventional life—weekends and evenings free to spend with your significant other, friends, and family—and *like* it that way.

- You want a career, not an adventure.

- There's a high degree of unpredictability—you'd rather not have your day (or week, or weekend, for that matter) change on a moment's notice thanks to the whims of your clients.

- You prefer being on the line and having profit-and-loss responsibility.

- You relish tangible, measurable work products, and results at the end of each day, week, and quarter—not Excel spreadsheets and PowerPoint slides.

- You prefer to work with one organization and see the fruits of your labor first-hand when the company implements your recommendations.

- Unstructured work with endless course corrections can be, well, annoying.

- You don't care for the consulting culture and its self-important people.

- You don't want the value of your contributions to be measured in billable hours.

- You don't feel that consultants add much value.

- Didn't get any callbacks.

And the Exceptions . . .

Even though the major pluses and minuses will be the same across the consulting board, there are a few key differences to keep in mind when you compare a career in HR, IT, or health care consulting with a career in strategy consulting.

Compensation. If tales of the sky-high salaries in consulting have been the primary driver of your interest in the field, keep in mind that total compensation is generally higher at strategy firms than elsewhere in the consulting industry. According to recent WetFeet research, 2005 undergraduates who landed consulting jobs received an average starting salary of $51,335; entry-level consultants at the top-tier strategy firms can earn compensation packages far north of that number. If you're considering a career in IT or HR consulting, the numbers are likely to be somewhat lower than that. "We're at a bit of a disadvantage when we recruit on-campus, because the starting salaries are considerably lower than at the strategy firms," says one of our insiders, who heads on-campus recruiting efforts for a leading HR consultancy.

Lifestyle. Many consulting insiders complain about the typical consulting lifestyle, which includes frequent travel, long hours, and a frustrating degree of unpredictability. But there are opportunities for consultants that are not typical. For example, one HR consulting firm insider mentioned that, as a whole, consultants at his organization travel less than ten percent of the time. "It's one of our major selling points," he says. "We tell people that they can feel free to actually rent an apartment, because they will be seeing that apartment on a regular basis." Depending on where you work, the hours also may be slightly more manageable than they would be at strategy firms. "If you want to work 80 or 90 hours a week, this isn't the place for you," says one insider at an industry-specific consulting practice. That said, keep in mind that hours in these areas of consulting will still be higher (on average) than comparable jobs in industry. As you consider different firms, be sure to ask how the lifestyle differs from that at other management consulting firms.

Brand-name recognition. If you're attracted to consulting because of the instant status it seems to afford those who do it, keep in mind that there will be fewer nods of recognition and awe if you work for a firm outside of the strategy ranks. The top HR consultancies, for example, are well known and instantly recognized within the consulting field, but they're far from household names (however, their clients often are).

CONSULTING OR INDUSTRY?

If you're thinking that you really aren't cut out to be a consultant, or if you're exploring other options, you might find this section helpful. We've tried to compare careers in consulting with their counterparts in industry. Although many graduates of top universities and MBA programs choose careers in the more glamorous consulting industry, most find work elsewhere. Given the seductive pull of the glitzy presentations given by consulting firms, chances are good that even if you're thinking about a career in industry, you may be tempted by the consulting world. To help you understand more about the difference, here's a summary of representative differences between the two options.

Industry Versus Consulting

Company	Consulting Firm
Work primarily with the same group of people	Project teams, colleagues, and clients change every few months
More direct involvement with a product	Arm's-length involvement with client's products
Make management decisions	Suggest management decisions
Deal with a wide range of people and have a direct impact on their daily lives	Deal mostly with senior and midlevel managers; have a large impact on regular people, but from a distance
Challenges revolve around getting things done, motivating people, dealing with personnel issues, making operating decisions	Challenges revolve around tackling and understanding complex problems and teaching clients to deal with them
Satisfaction from making product change	Satisfaction from affecting organization and competitiveness
Learn from a mentor with years of industry or functional experience	Learn from a mentor who is closer in age to you and who has consulting experience
With a good education and ambition, you might really stand out	With the most extraordinary accomplishments, you'll just be equal to everybody else
Your reputation and connections develop over months and years	Have to make quick impressions, then move on
Compensation packages generally lower, but you might get stock options	Compensation and perks more attractive

WHICH FIRMS ARE RIGHT FOR YOU?

If you're already set on a particular subset of consulting, the next question to consider is what type of firm presents the most promising opportunities for your personal and professional growth. How do you decide among the different types of firms? If you're interested in health care consulting, for example, how do you choose between a larger, diversified firm with a strong health care industry group (like Capgemini), a strategy consulting firm with a health care practice (like McKinsey), and a specialized health care consulting firm (like First Consulting Group, or the Lewin Group)? Here are some factors that should contribute to your decision:

Your Prior Professional Experience

Your work experience will determine what kind of firm you should target, particularly if you're looking to break into health care consulting or HR strategy consulting. As a general rule, specialist firms prefer to hire people with skills relevant to their specialty.

If you're hoping to land a job with a health care consulting practice, health care–specific work experience (with a hospital, government agency, or insurer/payer organization) will significantly advance your candidacy. If you're trying to break into health care consulting immediately after completing an undergraduate program, it will be difficult to specialize during your first few years on the job.

Human resources consulting firms, on the other hand, do hire candidates straight out of undergraduate programs, but they are more frequently hired into firms' actuarial or outsourcing practices. For their more strategic HR consulting work, these firms typically make lateral hires, either from other consulting firms or from HR departments within industry.

Your Education

Not surprisingly, firms that hire IT consultants look for candidates with technical educational backgrounds: Typically, candidates who are successful landing IT consulting jobs hold degrees in computer science, management information systems, or systems engineering. Candidates with degrees in mathematics, finance, or accounting—generally with work experience in IT—also tend to do well in the IT job search. Many firms that hire IT consultants conduct formal recruiting campaigns at undergraduate institutions. Since there are relatively few MBAs among the IT consulting ranks, firms tend not to recruit extensively at graduate business schools.

Among health care consultants, most competitive candidates hold one or more advanced degrees in health-related disciplines, and they often boast an educational background in business or economics as well. A cross section of senior professionals at one specialty firm offered academic credentials ranging from MDs, PhDs in economics, MBAs, and master's degrees in public policy and public health.

Because of their small size, firms that specialize in one industry or function are less likely to launch formal on-campus recruiting efforts, preferring instead to recruit on an as-needed basis from advanced-degree programs or other consulting firms.

 INSIDER TIP

If you have your eye on a particular industry or function, be aware that not all consulting firms use the same terminology—one firm's "e-commerce" practice may be another firm's "technology" practice, and one firm's "human resources" group may be called "talent and organizational change" somewhere else.

Your Goals and Priorities

Single-industry firms tend to be smaller and less well known to the broader business and consulting community than firms that support multiple industry practices, so if name-brand recognition is important to you, you may want to target larger, diversified practices.

You should also consider which training and development opportunities are critical to your career decision. Generally, the larger the consulting firm, the more likely it is to offer structured, formalized training programs for junior consultants. Your further education plans might also come into play; if you'd like to pursue an advanced degree at some point, many management consulting firms structure their analyst programs as two- or three-year commitments; at the end of these programs, many people choose to pursue an MBA or other advanced degree. If you'd prefer to stay with the firm, it's worth noting that IT and HR consulting positions offer more opportunities for promotion without an advanced degree.

The Firms

ACCENTURE

1345 Avenue of the Americas
New York, NY 10105
Phone: 917-452-4400
Fax: 917-527-9915
www.accenture.com
Ticker: ACN

A consulting behemoth, Accenture—formerly Andersen Consulting—started out as the consulting sibling of tax and accounting firm Arthur Andersen. In 1999, tired of having to share profits with its poor relation, Andersen Consulting asked for its independence. Arthur Andersen refused, and the case was submitted to an international arbitration court. The arbitrator put much of the blame for the split on Arthur Andersen, and ordered Andersen Consulting to give up its name and pay $1 billion in exchange for its independence, significantly less than the $14 billion Arthur Andersen wanted. In 2001, Accenture spent $175 million to reintroduce itself under its new name (which rhymes with "adventure" and is meant to convey the firm's "accent on the future") and went public. The timing couldn't have been more fortuitous—a short time later, Arthur Andersen imploded in the wake of the Enron scandal.

The firm's nearly 130,000 employees include more than 4,000 senior executives. Accenture has operations in more than 110 cities in 48 countries. Its client roster contains 87 of the Fortune Global 100, and nearly two-thirds of the Fortune Global 500.

Accenture's offerings include consulting services (with 10 practice areas, including change management, human resources management, and workplace performance), technology services (including enterprise integration, enterprise solutions, information management, infrastructure solutions, IT strategy and transformation, Microsoft solutions, mobile technology solutions, radio frequency identification, SAP solutions, service-oriented architecture, and systems integrations), and outsourcing services (including application outsourcing; BPO, which incorporates Accenture HR Services; and infrastructure outsourcing). It goes to market in 17 industry verticals, including Health and Life Sciences.

Accenture does business in three regions: the Americas; Europe, the Middle East, and Africa (EMEA); and the Asia Pacific. In 2005, its EMEA business accounted for about 50 percent of revenue, while the Americas accounted for 43 percent and the Asia Pacific for 7 percent. The firm is looking to expand its business in the Asia Pacific, hoping to take advantage of the growth of BPO operations in India, as well as expanding opportunities in China as that country increasingly opens its borders to foreign business operations. The firm beefed up its health care offerings substantially in 2005, with the acquisition of Capgemini's North American health care practice. Its 2006 acquisition of Pecaso, an IT company that specializes in SAP Human Capital Management integration and consulting, strengthened its HR-related offerings.

According to WetFeet research, typical undergrad Accenture salary offers in 2005 ranged from about $45,000 to $55,000, with typical signing bonuses in the $3,500 range. MBA offers were in the $95,000 to $120,000 range, with a typical signing bonus of around $8,000.

Key Financial Stats

2005 revenue: $17,094 million
1-year growth rate: 13 percent

Personnel Highlights

Number of employees: 123,000
1-year growth rate: 23 percent

Recent Highlights

2006   Announces partnership with Microsoft and Avanade to build integrated broad-cast system for MediaCorp.

Announces acquisition of Pecaso, an IT firm specializing in SAP Human Capital Management.

Acquires Savista's BPO assets.

Launches innovation center in India to support Oracle-related work in the region.

2005   Acquires Media Audits, which specializes in measuring ROI on advertising investments.

China Minsheng Banking Corporation signs Accenture and SAP to build its banking technology system.

Acquires Capgemini's North American health practice.

2004   Opens Guangzhou office in southern China.

Named Microsoft's 2004 global partner of the year.

Signs six-year, £400 million IT outsourcing contract with Barclays in the U.K.

Launches procurement BPO business.

Wins contract with U.S. Dept. of Homeland Security to create a new entry/exit system for the country's 400+ air, land, and sea ports of entry.

Buy the WetFeet Insider Guide to *Accenture* for more information about the firm.

AON CONSULTING WORLDWIDE

200 East Randolph Street, 10th floor
Chicago, IL 60601
Phone: 312-381-4844
Fax: 312-381-0240
www.aon.com
Ticker: AOC (parent organization)

Aon Consulting Worldwide is a subsidiary of the Aon Corporation, a Fortune Global 500 company that is the second largest insurance brokerage in the world after Marsh & McLennan. Aon Consulting is the human capital consulting division of the corporation. It operates 117 offices around the world. Its offerings include employee benefits; compensation and rewards; HR outsourcing; communication consulting; talent selection and development; business and HR alignment strategies; management consulting; mergers and acquisitions; workforce strategies; and specialized research. In 2006, Aon Consulting established a new financial advisory & litigation services practice.

The company employs people with a range of backgrounds, including actuarial science, business, employee benefits, compensation, industrial psychology, organizational behavior, HR information technology, employment compliance, process improvement design, communication, and leadership development. It goes to market in industry groups including financial services, government, health care, manufacturing, pharmaceuticals, the public sector, retail, and technology.

Aon Consulting named a new CEO, Kathryn Hayley, in 2006. She comes to the firm from Deloitte Consulting.

Key Financial Stats

2005 revenue: $1,255 million

1-year growth rate: not available

Personnel Highlights

Number of employees: 6,800

1-year growth rate: not available

Recent Highlights

2006   Sells compensation-data unit to Salary.com.

Names Kathryn Hayley new CEO in the United States.

Adds high-tech investigations, information security, and IT consulting to its financial advisory and litigation services practice.

Receives 2005 "Product of the Year" award from *Customer Inter@ction Solutions* magazine for its REPeValuator, a web-based sales, service, and collections tool.

2005   Partners with Ameriprise Retirement Services to offer comprehensive retirement plan solution for employers and employees.

Appoints Andrew M. Appel as CEO of Aon Consulting Worldwide.

Reorganizes HR outsourcing group to better integrate consulting and outsourcing services.

2004   Signs three-year deal to provide outsourced employment and staffing services for Cinergy.

Forms strategic alliance with Computer Sciences Corporation to develop and deliver human-resources business process outsourcing.

BAIN & COMPANY

131 Dartmouth Street
Boston, MA 02116
Phone: 617-572-2000
Fax: 617-572-2427
www.bain.com

Bain & Company is a leading strategy consulting firm with 32 offices in 20 countries. It provides strategic advice and recommendations for business problems to leading companies in virtually every economic sector. Bain was founded in 1973 by Bill Bain, a former VP at the Boston Consulting Group, and several others. Bain's capabilities include change management, corporate strategy, cost & supply chain management, growth strategy, IT (because it looks upon itself as a firm of generalists, Bain was relatively late to the tech consulting game), M&A, organization, performance improvement, private equity (it does a lot of business with private equity firms, and has benefited hugely from the growth in the private equity business in recent years), and revenue enhancement.

In the beginning, Bain distinguished itself by forging long-term relationships with clients by agreeing not to work with their competitors in exchange for reciprocal fidelity. In more recent times, Bain was one of the first consulting firms to link its pay to its client's performance.

The firm nearly went under in the late 1980s, when its debt load, a recession, and negative publicity resulting from a conflict of interest entered into by a Bain VP combined to put the firm on its heels. Bain sent its founder, Bill Bain, packing in 1991, and promoted Orit Gadiesh, one of the darlings of the consulting world, to run the show starting in 1993; since then, Bain's performance has been generally quite strong. Indeed, its current consultant headcount of 2,400 represents a growth of more than 400 percent from its 1991 consultant headcount of 550.

Bain's health care practice is especially strong. The firm has conducted more than 700 health care cases (that's what it calls its consulting engagements) for providers (hospitals and physicians), payers (insurance companies and HMOs), manufacturers (pharmaceutical and biotech companies), and distributors (sellers of medical equipment and supplies). These projects have encompassed corporate strategies, growth strategies, mergers and acquisitions, customer and loyalty management, and sales/channel management. The health care practice helps clients (which include for-profit, nonprofit, government, and academic organizations around the globe) to manage R&D, enter new markets, and improve operations.

Bain ranked fourth on the most recent *Fortune* list of companies "Where MBAs Most Want to Work." According to WetFeet research, in 2005 Bain offered undergrads coming on board a salary of $55,000, and a signing bonus of $4,000, while MBA offers ranged from $105,000 to $115,000, with a $15,000 signing bonus.

Key Financial Stats

Not available

Personnel Highlights

Number of consultants: 2,400
1-year growth rate: not available

Recent Highlights

2006   Names 20 new partners.

Bain consultant Ashish Singh named one of the industry's 25 top consultants by *Consulting Magazine*.

Deploys podcast to recruit students at the Indian Institute of Mangement.

2005   Makes top 10 on *Consulting Magazine*'s 2005 ranking of the "Best Consulting Firms to Work For."

Names eight new partners.

Announces plans to open a full-fledged consulting business in India in 2006.

2004   *Mastering the Merger*, a book by a couple of Bain consultants, is published.

Opens a "Capability Center" in Gurgaon, India.

Chairperson Orit Gadiesh named one of the "World's 100 Most Powerful Women" by *Forbes*.

Buy the WetFeet Insider Guide to *Bain & Company* for more information about the firm. And to find out how Bain describes itself, check out the free company interview at www.wetfeet.com.

BEARINGPOINT

1676 International Drive
McLean, VA 22102
Phone: 703-747-3000
Fax: 703-747-8500
www.bearingpoint.com
Ticker: BE

BearingPoint, formerly KPMG Consulting, is a system integrator, business advisor, and outsourcing services provider. The firm goes to market in a number of industries including banking, insurance, automotive, chemicals and natural resources, communications, consumer package goods, content, defense, education, electronics and software, government, health services, industrial markets, nonprofit, oil and gas, retail/wholesale, transportation, and utilities. Its offerings include CRM; enterprise resource planning (ERP); search solutions (it recently teamed with Google to launch this practice); supply chain management; technology infrastructure and integration; strategy, process, and transformation; finance; service-oriented architecture; and outsourcing (including HR business process outsourcing and IT outsourcing).

The firm traces its roots to 1870, when William Barclay Peat (the P in the former KPMG moniker) founded his London accounting firm. More than a century of mergers culminated in 1987, when Peat Marwick International and Klynveld Main Goerdeler merged to become a modern, world-class firm. The consulting arm separated from KPMG, its Big Four parent, in 2000. In 2001, KPMG Consulting went public, and in 2002 it changed its name to BearingPoint. It also went on an acquisition spree, adding practices and expanding around the world. Today, the firm has offices in more than 50 countries.

BearingPoint is a major player in the IT consulting sector, offering expertise in IT strategy, CRM applications, enterprise solutions, and technology integration. It recently introduced an outsourcing practice, bringing its portfolio of offerings in line with competitors such as Accenture and IBM.

In addition to its IT consulting success, BearingPoint is also a major player in the health services and life sciences sectors. The firm counts as clients six of the largest ten health systems and four of the five largest managed care organizations, as well as the largest 13 pharmaceutical companies in the Fortune 500. The company has been plagued of late by the need to restate its 2004 and 2005 performance due to accounting irregularities.

According to WetFeet research, in 2005 BearingPoint offered $45,000 in salary to undergrad hires, and $75,000 (plus a signing bonus in the $7,500 range) to MBA hires.

The firm looks for candidates with characteristics like leadership and teamwork skills and an entrepreneurial spirit ("How BearingPoint Pinpoints its MBAs," *Business Week* Online, 6/27/05). MBAs with an understanding of technology are particularly attractive to the firm.

Key Financial Stats

2004 revenue: $3,376 million
1-year growth rate: 8 percent

Personnel Highlights

Number of employees: 17,600
1-year growth rate: 17 percent

Recent Highlights

2006   Partners with Google to launch search solutions practice group.

Opens new software development center in Hattiesburg, Miss.

Launches technology showroom outside Washington, D.C. to showcase new, secure ID technologies it's developed.

2005   Wins USAID contracts for work in Afghanistan, Egypt, Montenegro, and Cyprus.

Wins contract to help New York and New Jersey improve port security.

Named one of the top ten health care consultants by *Modern Healthcare*.

Names Harry You CEO. Previously, he served as CFO at Oracle and at Accenture.

2004   Named software provider consultant of choice by Exelon.

Launches *Business Empowered*, a quarterly magazine focusing on business and technology issues facing chief executives, in partnership with *Forbes*.

BOOZ ALLEN HAMILTON

Corporate Headquarters:
8283 Greensboro Drive
McLean, VA 22102
Phone: 703-902-5000
Fax: 703-902-3333

Worldwide Commercial Business:
101 Park Avenue
New York, NY 10178
Phone: 212-697-1900
Fax: 212-551-6732

www.boozallen.com

Booz Allen Hamilton, one of the oldest and most prestigious firms in the consulting industry, is a major force both domestically and internationally, with about 60 offices in 29 countries. The firm is wholly owned by its 200-odd officers. Its areas of expertise include IT strategy & systems and organization. People & performance and healthcare & life sciences are among its practice areas. Booz does a whole lot of work for the government, which is probably the main reason its headquarters is located just outside Washington, D.C. Indeed, it's done quite a bit of defense- and national security–related work for the federal government in recent years.

Booz was founded in Chicago in 1914 by management consulting pioneer Edwin Booz. The firm started doing a lot of work for the government during World War II. By its 80th anniversary in 1994, its annual revenue had surpassed $950 million. The increasing importance of IT and government work have kept Booz on the growth track since then; in fiscal 2005, it posted revenue of $3.0 billion.

Booz Allen offers employees all sorts of programs and perquisites, and has a strong employment brand as a result. For instance, it ranked number 72 on the 2006 *Fortune* list of the "100 Best Companies to Work For," receiving special attention for its corporate university and its partnership with the Johns Hopkins MBA program. In 2005, *Washingtonian* magazine named Booz to its list of great places to work in the DC area, citing the fact that almost half of new hires at the firm come from employee referrals (which says a lot about what employees think of their employer), as well as the firm's contributions to and participation in the local community. In 2005 the firm also made the *Consulting Magazine* list of the "Top 10 Consulting Firms" and, for the seventh straight year, *Working Mother*'s list of the "100 Best Companies for Working Mothers."

According to WetFeet research, in 2005 Booz Allen offered incoming undergrads a salary of $55,000, while MBA offers ranged from $73,000 to $110,000 with an average signing bonus of around $10,000.

Key Financial Stats

2005 revenue: $3,000 million
1-year growth rate: 11 percent

Personnel Highlights

Number of employees: 17,000
1-year growth rate: 6 percent

Recent Highlights

2006   Ranks number 72 in this year's *Fortune* ranking of the "Best Companies to Work For."

Named "Most Valuable General Services Administration Schedule Contractor" by the Coalition for Government Procurement.

2005   Named a D.C.-area "Great Place to Work" by *Washingtonian* magazine.

2004   Selected as a prime contractor to USAID in support of commercial, legal, and institutional reforms and macroeconomic policy and development in developing countries.

Selected by National Institute of Child Health & Human Development to support a landmark study of the effects of environmental influences on the health and development of U.S. children.

Buy the WetFeet Insider Guide to *Booz Allen Hamilton* for more information about the company. And to find out how Booz Allen describes itself, check out the free company interview at www.wetfeet.com.

THE BOSTON CONSULTING GROUP

Exchange Place, 31st Floor
Boston, MA 02109
Phone: 617-973-1200
Fax: 617-973-1399
www.bcg.com

The Boston Consulting Group (BCG) is one of the top-tier management consulting firms. Founded in 1963, BCG came to prominence in the 1970s when it began challenging McKinsey & Company for high-level strategy work with large corporations. The firm has developed a number of analytical tools such as capability-driven competitive strategies and concepts such as total shareholder return, which are used throughout the consulting industry. BCG has always had a strong international presence; its second office was in Tokyo. Today, BCG has more than 50 offices in some 28 countries—and, while 11 of those offices are in the U.S., nearly two-thirds of its business comes from overseas work.

BCG offers a particularly strong health care industry group, with a reputation for its strategy capabilities in the sector. The firm derives a larger percentage of its revenue from non-U.S. operations than its closest strategy competitors, but it has been making progress breaking into the U.S. market over the past few years.

Aside from its sterling reputation as a strategic advisor, the company consistently earns recognition as an employer of choice—both inside and outside of the consulting ranks. In 2006 it ranked number 11 on *Fortune*'s list of the "100 Best Companies to Work For." The strength of its employment brand can be attributed at least in part to its tight-knit culture, which BCG works hard to maintain. Indeed, the firm keeps in touch with the vast majority of its alumni—a recent Alumni Day was attended by more than a third of BCG alumni in 60 cities around the world.

The firm values intelligence over specific technical knowledge in job candidates. For MBAs, the company focuses its recruiting efforts on Harvard, Stanford, Kellogg, the University of Chicago, Wharton, MIT's Sloan School of Management, Duke's Fuqua School of Business, Darden at the University of Virginia, and Dartmouth's Tuck School. It recruits undergrads at many of the same, and similar, schools. BCG places particular emphasis on the case interview, so candidates are advised to prepare well for those.

According to WetFeet research, in 2005 BCG offered undergrads coming on board a salary of $55,000 to $65,000, with an average signing bonus of $11,500. MBA offers ranged from $100,000 to $120,000 with an average signing bonus of $16,000.

Key Financial Stats

2005 revenue: $1,500 million
1-year growth rate: not available

Personnel Highlights

Number of consultants: 2,900
1-year growth rate: not available

Recent Highlights

2006   Ranks number 11 on *Fortune*'s 2006 list of the "Best Companies to Work For."

2005   Named one of the "10 Best Consulting Firms to Work For" by *Consulting Magazine*.

   BCG consultant Miki Tsusaka named to *Consulting Magazine*'s annual list of the "25 Top Consultants in the Business."

   Opens Detroit office.

2004   Sandy Moose, the consulting industry's first female consultant, retires from BCG after four decades in the industry.

Buy the WetFeet Insider Guide to *The Boston Consulting Group* for more information about the company.

CAPGEMINI

Place de l'Etoile
11, rue de Tilsitt
75017 Paris, France
Phone: +33-1-47-54-50-00
Fax: +33-1-47-54-50-86

U.S. Headquarters:
750 Seventh Avenue, Suite 1800
New York, NY 10019
Phone: 212-314-8000
Fax: 212-314-8001

www.capgemini.com

Capgemini, the largest supplier of information technology services in Europe, became the world's second-largest consulting practice when it acquired the management consulting side of Ernst & Young in May 2000. With the acquisition, Capgemini significantly increased its North American business, which now represents about 20 percent of its revenue.

Capgemini is organized into four areas of business: consulting (including HR consulting), technology, outsourcing (including HR and IT outsourcing), and local professional services (in the form of Sogeti/Transiciel, a wholly owned subsidiary of Capgemini, which provides IT services for small- and mid-sized projects in Europe and North America, contributing some 15 percent to Capgemini's total revenue). Health care and life sciences are among the 11 industries Capgemini serves, but it sold its North American health care practice to Accenture, for $175 million, in 2005.

The early 2000s were rough on Capgemini, and included revenue declines in many businesses and regions, largely due to having taken on the IT-focused E&Y consulting business just before the technology market began to stumble mightily. The technology market is on the rise these days, though, and Capgemini seems well-positioned to flourish if that rise continues. Major wins in recent times include a 10-year, $3.5 billion outsourcing deal it signed with energy giant TXU in 2004, and an outsourcing arrangement with the United Kingdom's Inland Revenue Service that, when it was signed, was the largest IT outsourcing contract anywhere in the world, worth about $5.3 billion over 8 to 10 years.

According to WetFeet research, in 2005 Capgemini entry-level MBA offers typically ranged from $96,000 to $106,000, with an average signing bonus of $12,000.

Key Financial Stats

2005 revenue: €6,954 million

1-year growth rate: 12 percent

Personnel Highlights

Number of employees (2004): 59,324

1-year growth rate: 19 percent

Recent Highlights

2006   Opens a third office in India, in Kolkata, which will initially focus on finance and accounting business process outsourcing, package implementation, and Web-based software development.

2005   Releases first business-focused Service-Oriented Architecture methodology into the public domain.

Salil Parekh is named general manager of North American Project and Consulting business.

Named "Outsourcing Service Provider of the Year" by the National Outsourcing Association.

Capgemini and SAP announce partnership in logistics service-providers industry.

2004   Extends global alliance with Microsoft to offer Microsoft technology solutions to clients across all industries worldwide.

Acquires Transiciel and combines it with its Sogeti subsidiary to form Sogeti/Transiciel, which provides systems integration and other IT services.

CONVERGYS CORPORATION

201 East 4th Street
Cincinnati, OH 45202
Phone: 513-723-7000
Fax: 513-421-8624
www.convergys.com
Ticker: CVG

Convergys Corporation provides consulting services, software support, and business process outsourcing (customer care and human resources services) in many industries, including communications, financial services, technology, and consumer products. Convergys, a member of the S&P 500, is headquartered in Cincinnati, Ohio, and has more than 65,000 employees in 72 customer contact centers, three data centers, and other facilities in the United States, Canada, Latin America, Europe, the Middle East, and Asia.

The company's fastest growing segment is the consulting and professional services unit, Convergys Professional Services, which grew by more than 30 percent in 2005. This unit focuses on business strategy and development, business process improvement, systems integration, and operations. Convergys consultants are based in various cities and regions throughout the world. Whenever possible, consultants are staffed to work at client sites in the city in which they live.

Convergys offers paid internships and co-op positions to qualified undergraduate and graduate candidates, and recruits at 15 U.S. universities.

Key Financial Stats

2005 revenue: $2,582 million
1-year change: 3.8 percent

Personnel Highlights

Number of employees: 66,300

1-year change: 16.9 percent

Recent Highlights

2006   Awarded "Best Overall Company" award at Telestrategies' Billing World 2006.

Signs multi-year agreement to provide outsourced billing and professional services to Disney Mobile.

2005   Names Dave Dougherty president and CEO.

Named to Fortune's list of "America's Most Admired Companies" for a fifth consecutive year; ranked number one among peers in innovation and social responsibility.

Becomes charter member of Technology Professional Services Association (TPSA).

ESPN Mobile selects Convergys to provide rating and billing software as well as professional and consulting services.

DuPont selects Convergys to provide transactional global human resource services.

2004   Expands professional services practice within its information management business by adding staff and technical capabilities such as custom development, integration planning, and implementation.

Selected to replace and consolidate billing systems with South America's largest wireless carrier, VIVO.

Acquires DigitalThink, expanding its learning outsourcing capabilities.

Acquires Finali Corporation, adding to its business transformation outsourcing services.

DELOITTE CONSULTING

1633 Broadway
New York, NY 10019
Phone: 212-489-1600
Fax: 212-489-1687
www.deloitte.com

Deloitte Consulting, along with Deloitte & Touche LLP (one of the Big Four accounting firms), is part of the global professional services organization Deloitte Touche Tohmatsu International. The firm offers its clients a selection of service lines that includes enterprise applications, human capital (its HR practice area, which includes specialty areas including actuarial & insurance solutions; change, leadership & learning; HR operations & technology; organization & people performance; total rewards; and talent management), outsourcing, strategy and operations, and technology integration. It focuses on nine industries: aviation and transport services; consumer businesses; energy and resources; financial services; life sciences and health care; manufacturing; the public sector; real estate; and technology, media, and communications.

Deloitte Consulting had a plan in place to separate from the tax and audit group and rename itself Braxton, after its strategy group, but the plans were abandoned in 2003, and Deloitte Consulting has since been reintegrated into the parent firm.

Deloitte is strong in all three areas this guide focuses on: human resources, health care, and technology. The firm consistently wins accolades for the work environment it offers employees, despite the lifestyle challenges inherent in a consulting career. In 2005, it made *Working Mother*'s annual list of the "100 Best Companies for Working Mothers" for the 12th straight year, ranked number six in *Training* magazine's annual list of top human capital development organizations, hit the top ten for the fourth straight year on *Latina Style*'s list of the "Top 50 companies for Latinas," and won the Silver Torch award from the National Association of Black MBAs for its commitment to diversity and inclusion.

According to WetFeet research, in 2005 Deloitte Consulting offered incoming under-grads a salary of $35,000 to $55,000, with an average signing bonus of $6,000. MBA offers ranged from $40,000 to $110,000 with an average signing bonus of $16,000.

Key Financial Stats

2005 revenue: $2,344 million

1-year growth rate: 14 percent

Personnel Highlights

Number of employees: 33,000

1-year growth rate: 12.3 percent

Recent Highlights

2006　Joins with Sun Microsystem to announce a collaborative initiative to help clients with regulatory compliance and technology governance.

Opens Center for Network Innovation in Washington, D.C. to help public- and private-sector clients better deal with integrating diverse technology systems.

Signs on as strategic sponsor of the Radio Frequency Identification (RFID) Research Center at the University of Arkansas' Information Technology Research Institute of the Sam M. Walton College of Business.

Two Deloitte consultants named to *Consulting Magazine*'s annual list of the 25 top consultants in the industry.

2004　Ranks number one among all outsourcing providers in an *Information Week* survey of 333 business-technology professionals.

Buy the WetFeet Insider Guide to *Deloitte Consulting* for more information about the company.

FIRST CONSULTING GROUP, INC.

111 West Ocean Boulevard
4th Floor
Long Beach, CA 90802
Phone: 562-624-5200
Fax: 562-432-5774
www.fcg.com
Ticker: FCGI

Of the top 75 management consulting firms in the world, First Consulting Group (FCG) is one of the few that serves the health care and life sciences industries exclusively. It offers consulting, technology, applied research, and outsourcing services through four primary business units. These business units correspond to the types of clients that FCG serves: health care providers, health plan insurers, government health care, and life sciences companies. (Of these business units, the life sciences practice is not the strongest.)

FCG's services include network engineering, application development, inbound and outbound call center services, IT staffing, and project management. FCG also provides systems development and integration, data warehousing, and IT outsourcing. In addition to technology consulting, FCG offers consulting in the areas of clinical drug development, business process and strategy, care management, and patient safety. In 2005, it saw growth in its Health Delivery Outsourcing, Government and Technology Services, and Health Plan businesses, while its Health Delivery Services and Life Sciences businesses both shrank. Growth was particularly strong in the Health Delivery Outsourcing business, which saw revenue rise more than 14 percent, to about $114 million (nearly 40 percent of total FCG revenue that year).

The company boasts both an impressive client roster and enviable customer satisfaction statistics. Among its current or former clients are 17 of the top 20 managed care firms and all of the leading pharmaceutical and life sciences companies listed in the *Forbes Global 500*. The firm ranked number 25 in *Healthcare Informatics'* 2005 list of "100 Leading Healthcare IT Companies."

Key Financial Stats

2005 revenue: $293 million

1-year growth rate: 2 percent

Personnel Highlights

Number of employees: 2,681

1-year growth rate: 10 percent

Recent Highlights

2006   Signs a two-year, $9.2 million systems integration contract with Oregon-based PacificSource Health Plans.

2005   CEO Luther J. Nussbaum resigns.

Loses UMass Memorial Health Care IT outsourcing contract, which was supposed to last for seven years when it went into effect in 2002.

Named one of more than 30 IT vendors designing the $18.6 million Nationwide Health Information Network for the U.S. Health and Human Services Department.

Launches FirstDoc 3.3 enterprise content management platform for the life sciences industry.

2004   Completes acquisition of Codigent Solutions Group, "a Nashville, Tenn.–based provider of value-added information technology solutions to hospitals and other healthcare delivery organizations."

Launches FirstGateways product, a Web-based tool for health care clinicians.

GARTNER, INC.

56 Top Gallant Road
Stamford, CT 06902
Phone: 203-964-0096
Fax: 866-618-0806
www.gartner.com
Ticker: IT

Gartner is—quite literally—a research firm first and a consulting firm second. The company (which celebrated its 25th anniversary in 2004) is a leading provider of research and analysis on the global information technology industry, and its goal is to support its client enterprises as they drive innovation and growth through the use of technology. First and foremost, the company helps its clients make informed technology and business decisions by providing in-depth analysis—based on independent and objective research—on virtually all aspects of technology.

Gartner's independent research is the fundamental building block for all Gartner services. The findings from this research can be delivered through several different media depending on a client's specific business needs, preferences, and objectives. Through Gartner Intelligence, the company offers content and advice for IT professionals, technology companies, and technology investors in the form of research reports, briefings, or events. Gartner's analysts provide in-depth analysis on virtually all aspects of technology and telecommunications, including hardware, software and systems, services, IT management, market data and forecasts, and industry-specific issues. The firm offers about 50 conferences around the world each year, attracting about 30,000 executives.

In addition to its research and analysis, Gartner offers peer networking services and membership programs designed specifically for CIOs and other senior executives as well as customized consulting services that leverage findings from the company's research. Gartner consulting services typically focus on outsourcing and IT management. Unlike many IT services firms, Gartner does not offer implementation services that would compromise its independence and objectivity.

In 2005, Gartner acquired the META Group, another IT research and consulting organization. Today it has about 3,700 associates, including roughly 650 research analysts and 550 consultants in 75 countries, and has a client base of some 10,000 organizations.

Key Financial Stats

2005 revenue: $989 million
1-year growth rate: 11 percent

Personnel Highlights

Number of employees: 3,622
1-year growth rate: 0 percent

Recent Highlights

2006   Launches Gartner for IT Leaders offering, which allows clients to more easily access the Gartner people and information they need.

2005   Expands IT outsourcing benchmarking solutions capabilities with new offering focuses on best practices in outsourcing contracts.

Establishes a wholly foreign-owned enterprise in Beijing.

Acquires META Group, an information technology research and consulting firm.

Increases presence in Spain and Portugal.

2004   COO leaves Gartner, and CEO Gene Hall assumes direct responsibility for operations.

Hires Bob Patton as president of Gartner Consulting.

HAY GROUP INC.

The Wanamaker Building
100 Penn Square East
Philadelphia, PA 19107
Phone: 215-861-2000
Fax: 215-861-2111
www.haygroup.com

The Hay Group is a research-driven HR consulting firm that advises its clients on the best ways to organize, manage, and reward their employees. The company offers ten service lines: performance management, job evaluation, organization effectiveness, talent management, capability assessment, reward strategies, executive rewards, leadership transformation, reward information services, and employee & customer surveys.

In many cases, Hay is brought in to help executive teams manage through major events, such as mergers, changes in strategy, and corporate restructuring. In other cases, senior leadership might bring in Hay to solve internal problems, such as turf wars and accountability problems.

Over the course of its more than 60-year history, the Hay Group has developed a number of proprietary tools that it uses to help its clients develop more effective workforces. Its Hay Group PayNet, for example, is an online tool that provides subscribers full access to Hay's compensation databases; subscribers can create custom queries based on a specific organization's industry, geography, or peer group across the jobs, families, and compensation elements desired. The company also developed EI (emotional intelligence) services to help employees improve their interpersonal effectiveness in the workplace. In addition to these tools, Hay provides one-on-one executive coaching for entire teams or individuals.

Hay is an international company with 2,000 employees working from 82 offices in 47 countries around the world. Although it works across industries with some 7,000 clients around the world, the company has built up substantial expertise in chemicals, consumer products, financial services, government, health care, manufacturing, pharmaceuticals, retail, and utilities.

According to industry insiders, the company's reputation among MBA candidates has lagged after several consecutive years of flat to negative growth. Some say that reviving its reputation on campus will be critical to Hay's future success.

Key Financial Stats

Not available

Personnel Highlights

Number of professionals: 2,000
1-year growth rate: not available

Recent Highlights

2006   For a ninth year, compiles *Fortune*'s rankings of the World's and America's "Most Admired Companies."

2005   Two Hay Group consultants named by FEM/Business, a Dutch management publication, among the 25 most influential Dutch consultants.

Partners with *Chief Executive* magazine to name "The Best Companies for Leaders."

Opens new offices in India, Israel, South Africa, and South Korea.

2004   Hay Group consultant named to *Consulting Magazine*'s list of the "25 Top Consultants in the Industry."

Hay Group founder is awarded WorldatWork's Keystone Award.

HEWITT ASSOCIATES

100 Half Day Road
Lincolnshire, IL 60069
Phone: 847-295-5000
Fax: 847-295-7634
www.hewitt.com

Hewitt Associates is a provider of HR outsourcing (which accounts for more than two-thirds of the firm's revenue) and consulting services (which account for the other third). The company's core HR outsourcing services include actuarial services for sponsors of retirement plans and executive compensation consulting. In addition, the company offers its Total Benefit Administration system for outsourcing the administration of the three major benefit service areas in an integrated fashion. Benefits outsourcing includes health and welfare (medical plans), defined contribution (401(k)) plans, and defined benefit (pension) plans. The company offers its outsourcing services primarily to large companies with complex benefit programs, including Marriott International, Home Depot, Coca Cola, UPS, and BellSouth.

Hewitt's consulting business covers a variety of services including health and welfare, compensation and retirement plans, and HR programs and processes. Its client list includes some 2,600 organizations, including more than half of the Fortune 500 and one-third of the Fortune Global 500.

In 2004, the company made headlines when it merged with Exult Inc., a leading provider of HR business process outsourcing, for $691 million in stock. As a result of the merger, Hewitt is now the global leader in the rapidly growing HR BPO industry. It believes its integration of HR consulting expertise and HR BPO capability gives it a unique competitive advantage.

According to WetFeet research, in 2005 Hewitt offered undergrads coming on board a salary of $40,000 to $45,000.

Key Financial Stats

2005 revenue: $2,899 million

1-year growth rate: 28 percent

Personnel Highlights

Number of employees: 22,000

1-year growth rate: 29 percent

Recent Highlights

2006   Partners with United Healthcare, Optima Health, Exante, and Intuit to develop new health care–focused software bearing the Quicken brand.

Opens HR outsourcing center in Poland.

Signs ten-year deal to provide HR business process outsourcing services for Catholic Health Initiatives.

2005   Names Bryan J. Doyle president of outsourcing business and Perry O. Brandorff president of consulting business.

CFO resigns and is replaced by Orbitz' CFO, John Park.

Acquires Royal Philips Electronics' pension administration arm.

2004   Launches Flexible Spending Account administration business.

Makes Fortune's list of America's most admired companies.

Merges with Exult, an HR business process outsourcing provider; the combined company is the world's biggest HR business process outsourcing provider.

IBM GLOBAL SERVICES

International Business Machines Corporation
New Orchard Road
Armonk, NY 10504
Phone: 914-499-1900
Fax: 914-765-7382
www.ibm.com/services

IBM may be better known for its computer hardware (though it shed its PC business in 2005, selling it to the Chinese firm Lenovo, it still does huge business in mainframes, servers, storage systems, peripherals, and semiconductors), but Big Blue's largest division is Global Services, which competes with the likes of Accenture, EDS, and HP Services. Indeed, it's currently the largest technology services organization in the world. Originally, IBM ran a consulting unit under the name IBM Consulting, but in 2000, it merged that group with its systems integration group to provide end-to-end business solutions. In 2002, IBM acquired PricewaterhouseCoopers' 30,000-employee-strong consulting and IT services business. PwC brought a client roster that included about 45 percent of the Fortune 500; higher-margin consulting skills; and experience in financial services, government, and consumer products that expanded IBM Global Services's expertise and capabilities. Health care is among the 20 industry verticals in which the firm goes to market.

Now, IBM Global Services operates in three broad areas: outsourcing, consulting, and system integration. In short, it can advise clients on devising e-commerce and supply management systems and enterprise resource planning, and then it can implement and manage those systems. In 2005, Global Services made up 52 percent of IBM's overall revenue. Much of the division's growth can be attributed not only to its BPO contracts, but to its business transformation outsourcing (BTO) contracts as well. BTO takes BPO one step further, giving client companies the opportunity to achieve significant business change—not just cost savings—through the use of technology. The company's sales of BTO services and related software totaled $4 billion in 2005, up 28 percent over 2004, and BPO revenue overall was up a whopping 144 percent ("Big Blue Is in the Pink," *BusinessWeek* Online, 1/18/06).

IBM ranked number 23 on *Fortune*'s 2006 list of the companies MBAs most want to work for. According to WetFeet research, in 2005 IBM offered undergrads coming on board a salary in the $44,000 to $55,000 range, with an average signing bonus of $1,500, while MBA offers ranged from $60,000 to $105,000, with an average signing bonus of $6,000. An IBM recruiter recently told *BusinessWeek*: "We hire MBAs into a variety of different functions in business consulting services, strategy and change, and IT consulting practices. We hire finance majors into a rotational program, and strong marketing MBAs get the opportunity to complete a leadership-development program in their function. We also find that MBAs make good business-development professionals… We recruit heavily from the University of Notre Dame Mendoza College of Business. We also hire MBAs from Emory University Goizueta Business School, MIT Sloan School of Management, Northwestern University Kellogg School of Management, Thunderbird Garvin School of International Management, University of Pennsylvania Wharton School, and a bunch of others" ("Big Traits for Big Blue," *BusinessWeek* Online, August 2005).

Key Financial Stats

2005 revenue: $47,357 million
1-year growth rate: 3 percent

Personnel Highlights

Number of employees (2004): 175,000
1-year growth rate: –2.8 percent

Recent Highlights

2006   Opens new Global Business Solution Center in Bangalore, India.

Carnegie Mellon University honors IBM with highest business transformation outsourcing group rating.

Collaborates with Scripps Research Institute to study pandemic viruses.

Announces it's making a $1 billion investment over three years to expand information management software development, and further aligning its software and consulting businesses.

2005   Extends lead in outsourcing, according to IDC report, capturing 21 of the 100 biggest deals of 2004.

Launches consulting practice aimed at helping clients deal with executive turnover as baby boomers leave the workforce.

Opens new global services delivery center in Dalian, China.

2004   IDC report names IBM Global Services leading firm for Web services.

Announces that it is investing $250 million over three years to beef up its health care business by creating new technology solutions, developing new partnerships, and making key hires.

MCKINSEY & COMPANY

55 East 52nd Street, 21st Floor
New York, NY 10022
Phone: 212-446-7000
Fax: 212-446-8575
www.mckinsey.com

McKinsey & Company is perhaps the most famous consulting firm in the world. The firm has a long history of providing strategic advice to the top management of the world's largest corporations. McKinsey was founded in 1926 when James O. McKinsey teamed up with partner Andrew T. Kearney to form a business advisory service. They were later joined by Marvin Bower, a Harvard MBA who went on to actively manage the firm for more than 30 years. McKinsey is renowned for its strict business standards, its strong culture, and for the breadth and depth of its experience base. It's known to charge among the highest fees for its work, and among consultants, McKinsey is the gold standard by which reputation and success are measured.

From 1994 to 2001, the firm more than doubled in both consultants and revenue, but it struggled along with the market in the early 2000s, laying off consultants and watching revenue fall. In November 2003, some associates reported that the road to partner track had been lengthened and a salary cap placed on the principal level. Still, the firm ranked number one in the most recent *Fortune* list of the "100 Companies MBAs Most Want to Work For."

McKinsey is a major player in health care consulting. Through its pharmaceuticals and medical products industry group, McKinsey focuses on large-scale strategy and operational projects. Roughly 30 percent of its health care work focuses on operational issues. Insiders suggest that the firm will become increasingly focused on its IT and operations consulting practices in the next few years.

According to WetFeet research, in 2005 McKinsey offered incoming undergrads a salary in the $55,000 to $65,000 range, with an average signing bonus of $6,500. MBA offers ranged from $75,000 to $120,000, with an average signing bonus of $17,500.

Key Financial Stats

2003 revenue: $3,000 million (est.)

1-year growth rate: not available

Personnel Highlights

Number of consultants: 6,000

1-year growth rate: not available

Recent Highlights

2006   Ranks first in Universum list of most popular employers for MBAs, for the 11th straight year.

Advises Dartmouth College on ways the school can better support faculty and students.

2005   Retained by News Corp. to help that company come up with a new Internet strategy.

Reuters reports that McKinsey plans to add some 700 employees in Asia over the next two years.

Aon poaches a McKinsey senior partner, Andrew Appel, to become CEO of Aon Consulting Worldwide.

Named one of the "10 Best Consulting Firms to Work For" by *Consulting Magazine*.

2004   Among the winners in the Global Most Admired Knowledge Enterprise awards, given out by knowledge management research company Teleos.

Buy the WetFeet Insider Guide to *McKinsey & Company* for more information about the firm.

MERCER HUMAN RESOURCE CONSULTING

1166 Avenue of the Americas
New York, NY 10036
Phone: 212-345-7000
Fax: 212-345-7414
www.mercerhr.com

Mercer, Inc., a subsidiary of Marsh & McLennan Companies, is one of the largest consulting firms in the world, with offices in 190 cities in 41 countries. Mercer Human Resource Consulting is one of Mercer's eight distinct divisions (other divisions include Mercer Management Consulting and National Economic Research Associates—better known as NERA).

The HR practice employs about 15,700 consultants worldwide and offers advisory services in all areas of HR consulting, from compensation and benefits to operational effectiveness and employee performance and engagement.

Mercer is still recovering from a series of blows to its reputation that started in 2004, when the SEC started investigating the firm over alleged "pay to play" tactics (i.e., getting investment managers to fork over large fees in exchange for Mercer's recommendation of those managers to pension funds). When New York State Attorney General Elliot Spitzer investigated the 2003 pay package to New York Stock Exchange CEO, Dick Grasso, which totaled $139.5 million, Mercer admitted that the report it prepared on Grasso's pay contained "omissions and inaccuracies." Mercer returned more than $400,000 in fees it collected from the NYSE for its work involving Grasso. The bad news for Mercer continued when, in 2005, its parent Marsh & McLennan agreed to settle charges brought by Spitzer's office that it rigged bids and fixed prices. Marsh restructured its operations in response to all the turmoil, making its Putnam Investments subsidiary (which was itself implicated in the recent mutual-fund industry scandals) more independent to avoid conflicts of interest when Mercer makes fund recommendations to clients, and integrating its Marsh brokerage unit with Mercer to cut costs and try to create cross-selling opportunities.

Mercer has been expanding of late, both organically, especially in the Asia Pacific region, and via acquisitions; recent additions include Watson Wyatt's New Zealand operations and Synhrgy HR Technologies.

Key Financial Stats

2005 revenue: $2,708 million
1-year growth rate: 0 percent

Personnel Highlights

Number of employees: 16,000
1-year growth rate: not available

Recent Highlights

2006   Named "Benefits Consultant of the Year" in annual Global Pensions Awards for the second straight year.

Announces expansion of compensation co-sourcing services in Singapore and the Asia Pacific region.

Opens office in Dalian, China.

Launches Mercer Retirement Solutions outsourcing business to serve defined contribution and defined benefit plan sponsors.

Combines its health care and group benefits businesses with those of Marsh, forming Mercer Health & Benefits LLC.

Forms Mercer HR Services to provide clients with outsourcing services.

Brian Storms named president and CEO of Mercer HR Consulting.

2004   Acquires Synhrgy HR Technologies.

MILLIMAN, INC.

1301 5th Avenue
Suite 3800
Seattle, WA 98101
Phone: 206-624-7940
Fax: 206-340-1380
www.milliman.com

Milliman Global is an international organization made up of consulting and actuarial firms located all over the world. The consulting firms together cover employee benefits, insurance, health care, and investment markets. Within the employee benefits market, Milliman provides solutions for HR issues such as pensions, compliance and reporting, employee communications, and international mergers. Milliman's health care services cover product design and development, claim costs, regulatory compliance, and public policy strategies. Milliman's specialty within the consulting market is, of course, on serving those businesses that have a scope that only a global company could serve; thus Milliman's primary base of clients consists mostly of multinationals and governments that need expertise on international as well as local issues.

Milliman, Inc., a U.S.-based consulting and actuarial firm within the larger Milliman Global network, offers its services to corporations, government entities, and financial institutions. Consultancy practice areas include health care, property and casualty insurance, employee benefits, and investment consulting. Its employee benefits group has a proven track record of pioneering work in defined benefit pensions, leading multi-employer and public plan practices, and a rapidly expanding 401(k) administration and investment consulting practice.

The company employs more than 1,900 individuals worldwide. It's owned by its more than 250 partners.

Key Financial Stats

2005 revenue: $435 million

1-year growth rate: not available

Personnel Highlights

Number of employees: 1,900

1-year growth rate: not available

Recent Highlights

2006   Parent company Milliman Global announces 2005 revenue of $579 million.

James Shibanoff, who edits the Milliman Care Guidelines and is considered to be a leader in the evidence-based medicine movement, is named one of the nation's 50 most influential physician executives by *Modern Physician* magazine.

2005   Acquires IntelRx, a provider of underwriting tools for insurers.

Opens offices in Warsaw and Munich.

2004   *True Group Long-Term Care*, a book by a couple of Milliman Consultants, is published.

Acquires Denver-based small-business retirement plan practice of Ceridian.

Milliman and *Employee Benefits News* magazine join forces to offer BenPulse, a comprehensive benefits survey and analysis benchmarking tool that allows companies to compare their individual and overall benefits against other companies' programs.

NAVIGANT CONSULTING, INC.

615 North Wabash Avenue
Chicago, IL 60611
Phone: 312-573-5600
Fax: 312-573-5678
www.navigantconsulting.com
Ticker: NCI

Formerly known as The Metzler Group, Navigant is a global consulting firm serving Fortune 500 companies, government agencies, law firms, and companies in regulated industries in areas including dispute, financial, regulatory, and operational advisory services. It has offices in 41 countries, including overseas offices in the Czech Republic, London, China, and Canada.

Through its health care practice, Navigant Consulting works with health care providers, payers, and life science companies to help improve their strategic, operational, and financial performance. Its clients include hospitals, health systems, physician practices, health plans, managed care organizations, pharmaceutical companies, biotech companies, medical device manufacturers, bond insurers, state and federal government agencies, corporate legal departments, and law firms. Professionals in Navigant's health care vertical include individuals with experience as hospital, health plan, and health care financing program executives as well as CPAs, PhDs, MDs, RNs, and many other clinical professionals.

The company has pursued an aggressive growth-via-acquisition strategy in recent years. Its acquisitions since 2001 include Barrington Energy Partners (an energy financial advisory services provider); the Hunter Group (health care provider interim management and performance improvement); teams from Arthur D. Little (Advanced Energy Systems and Technology Innovation Management) and Arthur Andersen, LLP (Litigation and Investigations and Government Contracting); Tucker Alan (litigation and investigations, construction, and healthcare consulting); Capital Advisory Services (finance and accounting process and systems consulting); Invalesco (healthcare patient throughput services); KI Solutions (information management consulting); Casas, Benjamin & White (middle-market M&A and restructuring financial advisory services); The Tiber Group; A.W. Hutchison & Associates; and Kroll Lindquist Avey Canada (Forensic Accounting and Litigation Consulting Practices).

Key Financial Stats

2005 revenue: $576 million
1-year growth rate: 19 percent

Personnel Highlights

Number of employees: 2,276
1-year growth rate: 11 percent

Recent Highlights

2006 Names Julie Howard president and CEO.

2005 Ranks number 58 in *Business Week*'s list of the "100 Best Small Companies."

2004 Acquires Invalesco Group, which provides patient throughput optimization and workflow solutions to health care provider organizations.

   Navigant consultant William Goodyear named to *Consulting Magazine*'s annual list of the "25 Top Consultants in the Industry."

NOVELL INC.

404 Wyman Street
Suite 500
Waltham, MA 02451
Phone: 781-464-8000
Fax: 782-464-8100
www.novell.com

Novell Inc. is a provider of network management software and network operating systems. The company's NetWare product, for example, enables organizations to connect individual desktops to entire corporate networks, while integrating things like directories, storage systems, printers, and databases—all of the individual pieces of a company's information infrastructure—into one seamless, secure system.

Over the past several years, the company has been realigning its strategy to focus on software for the Linux platform and identity management technology—basically, betting the house on the open-source software revolution. Its technology offerings include data center, security and identity, resource management, workgroup, and desktop solutions. It also offers training and consulting services to support the technologies it sells, with consulting expertise in strategy and architectures, solution design and deployment, training-needs assessment and skills development, and solution support. Its partner ecosystem includes a broad range of hardware and software vendors, consultants, and system integrators.

Novell operates through four business segments: systems, security, and identity management; open-platform solutions; workplace solutions; and Celerant Management Consulting, which provides management consulting services through its offices in Europe and the United States. Celerant, which is separate from Novell's consulting offerings in the support technologies it sells, helps clients in 11 industry groups (including life sciences and health care) improve their organizational effectiveness, manage technology implementation, and streamline their supply chain systems. The firm also provides Six Sigma implementation and training services. (Six Sigma is an efficiency-maximization methodology made famous by General Electric's Jack Welch.) Celerant's customers have included BP, Church & Dwight, and RadioShack.

Novell offers its software products and consulting services through its 40 offices around the world.

In 2001, Novell acquired Cambridge Technology Partners, a consulting firm that made a name for itself by helping companies navigate successful transitions into the electronic marketplace. Novell's acquisition of Cambridge Technology Partners significantly expanded its ability to deliver consulting support to customers and other IT services companies. Cambridge combined its expertise in financial services, communications, energy, and manufacturing to Novell's existing platform in business, government, and education markets.

Key Financial Stats

2005 revenue: $1,198 million
1-year growth rate: 3 percent

Personnel Highlights

Number of employees: 5,066
1-year growth rate: −18 percent

Recent Highlights

2006   Launches SUSE Linux Enterprise, its latest (and most sophisticated) version of a Linux desktop.

      Partners with IBM to offer a suite of products to help small- and medium-sized businesses more easily implement Linux.

      The Novell-sponsored openSUSE project is named Best in Show as a total industry solution at LinuxWorld Conference & Expo in Boston.

2005   Acquires Immunix, a provider of Linux security solutions.

Signs major deal with U.S. Dept. of Health and Human Services, giving employees unlimited access to a range of Novell products.

Opens a number of offices in China.

Announces it's restructuring and laying off some ten percent of its workforce.

Launches new partner program in India to promote the use of Novell/SUSE Linux solutions among retailers, distributors, channel partners, consultants, and system integrators.

2004   Begins offering SUSE Linux customers legal protection for using the open-source operating system.

TOWERS PERRIN

One Stamford Plaza
263 Tresser Boulevard
Suite 700
Stamford, CT 06901
Phone: 203-326-5400
Fax: 203-326-5499
www.towersperrin.com/hrservices/global/default.htm

Towers Perrin operates three main lines of business: HR Services, Reinsurance, and Tillinghast (which, among other things, provides software and consulting to insurance and financial services companies).

The HR Services business of Towers Perrin provides global HR consulting and administration services that help organizations effectively manage their investment in people. It offers its clients consulting services in areas such as employee benefits, compensation, communication, change management, employee research, and HR service delivery (i.e., outsourcing of retirement, health and welfare plans, and compensation administration). Insiders predict that the company's growing market share in the outsourcing market should afford it ample cross-selling opportunities for its consulting services.

Towers Perrin has streamlined its operations in recent times, focusing on bigger customers while launching new practices in areas like public relations and corporate communications. Its clients include three-quarters of the world's 500 largest companies and three-quarters of the Fortune 1000. Across all of its business units, Towers Perrin has more than 7,500 employees in 25 countries.

According to WetFeet research, in 2005 Towers Perrin offered undergrad hires an average salary of $45,000, with a signing bonus around $5,000. MBA offers ranged from $85,000 to $110,000, with an average signing bonus of $5,000.

Key Financial Stats

2004 revenue: $1,620 million

1-year growth rate: 8 percent

Personnel Highlights

Number of employees: 7,827

1-year growth rate: –7 percent

Recent Highlights

2006   Partners with Greco International, an actuary and benefits-consulting firm that serves clients in Austria, Hungary, the Czech Republic, and Slovenia; and Polish companies Trio Management, an employee-benefits and actuarial consultancy, and HRK Partners, an HR consultancy, to extend its reach in central and eastern Europe.

Acquires Risk Capital Management Partners, a financial risk-management consulting firm serving the financial services, energy, utilities, and mining industries.

Releases "A Problem in Search of Solutions: A Study of Defined Benefit Pensions" research report.

2005   Launches ExcellerateHRO, a joint venture with EDS that provides comprehensive HR outsourcing and consulting services to worldwide organizations.

Forms alliance with Cerebrus Consultants, an HR consulting firm, in India.

Releases largest single study of the worldwide workplace, surveying "more than 85,000 people working for large and midsize companies in 16 countries on four continents."

Announces the Rx Collaborative, a coalition bringing together more than 30 big employers to achieve lower drug-pricing costs.

UNISYS

Unisys Way
Blue Bell, PA 19424
Phone: 215-986-4011
Fax: 215-986-2312
www.unisys.com

Unisys is an IT giant, with offerings including consulting, systems integration, outsourcing, infrastructure, and server technology, in the following markets: financial services, public sector, communications, transportation, commercial, and media. The company is among the largest government IT contractors, serving local, state, and federal agencies, as well as foreign governments. Unisys has offices in 36 U.S. states 65 countries around the world.

Like many of its competitors, the company has been growing its outsourcing business in recent years; outsourcing currently accounts for nearly a third of Unisys's total revenue. Unisys has signed outsourcing deals with clients including Lloyds TSB, Northwest Airlines, Air Canada, California State University Systems, BMW Bank, HSBC, and GE Capital Bank. The company's current strategy aims to take advantage of growth in software markets including open-source software and security.

Key Financial Stats

2005 revenue: $5,759 million
1-year growth rate: −1 percent

Personnel Highlights

Number of employees: 36,100
1-year growth rate: −3 percent

Recent Highlights

2006   Announces new China global sourcing services and technology center in Shanghai.

       Awarded a bridge contract to continue work on the technology infrastructure of the Transportation Security Administration of the Department of Homeland Security.

2005   Wins Qualcomm 3G A-List Award for its use of Qualcomm technology among its 1,700 North America–based field reps to lower costs and improve customer service.

       Introduces on-demand servers for Windows and Linux.

       Wins national claims outsourcing services contract with Blue Cross/Blue Shield.

2004   Acquires Baesch Computer Consulting, which serves U.S. intelligence and defense organizations.

WATSON WYATT WORLDWIDE, INC.

901 North Glebe Road
Arlington, VA 22203
Phone: 703-258-8000
Fax: 703-258-8585
www.watsonwyatt.com
Ticker: WW

Watson Wyatt Worldwide is a global consulting firm specializing in human capital and financial management. The company is one of the largest HR consulting firms, with practices in communication, compensation, government consulting, health care, human capital consulting, insurance and financial services, international (which serves multinational corporations and their overseas subsidiaries), investment consulting, organization effectiveness and development, pensions administration, retirement, technology solutions, and tools and technology. The company has nearly 3,900 employees in 92 offices in 31 countries.

Watson Wyatt is also recognized for the quality of its research and thought leadership. For example, the company developed the Human Capital Index (HCI), a methodology used to calculate the correlation between human capital and shareholder value. The index quantifies exactly which HR practices and policies contribute most significantly to shareholder value, enabling client organizations to prioritize possible HR initiatives.

There have been rumors in recent years that the company may be a takeover target; without a significant outsourcing practice, industry experts say the firm repeatedly loses business to competitors, and they suspect that Watson Wyatt will either have to acquire or be acquired to remain competitive. IBM and Accenture have both been mentioned as potential suitors.

Key Financial Stats

2005 revenue: $737 million

1-year growth rate: 5 percent

Personnel Highlights

Number of employees: 3,875

1-year growth rate: −1 percent

Recent Highlights

2006   Forms partnership with software company Quest Analytics to help clients better understand health care provider quality.

Appoints Kevin Meehan U.S. region manager.

Opens Frankfurt office.

2005   Acquires Chicago actuarial and benefits consultant Davis, Conder, Enderle & Sloan.

Acquires European sister company Watson Wyatt LLP.

Opens Las Vegas office.

Opens office in Chile and research center in Uruguay.

2004   Opens insurance and financial services practice in Munich.

Sets up research and information center in Singapore.

On the Job

The Engagement

Key Jobs

Real People Profiles

The Engagement

In a nutshell, consultants are hired advisors to the world's largest and most powerful organizations. In this role, they tackle a variety of issues, all of which ultimately boil down to a few central themes. Consultants define problems, develop methodologies for solving problems, collect data that will help solve problems, and—you guessed it—solve problems. In our overviews of consulting in each of the HR, IT, and health care sectors, we provided examples of the types of engagements (or projects, or cases, depending on the terminology used by the specific firms) that consultants in each of these areas might work on. In this section, we give you a sense of the day-to-day mechanics of a consulting engagement: characteristics of the work environment that tend to be relatively consistent from firm to firm and practice area to practice area.

PROJECT CYCLE

A typical consulting engagement can last anywhere from one month to several years. In general, however, industry insiders note that the typical tenure of a consulting project has fallen from 6 to 18 months in the 1990s to as little as a month or two currently. This trend makes sense given that organizations have less money to spend on big consulting engagements and that clients want better, faster results, and they're demanding a tangible return on investment from the consulting services they buy.

During a consulting engagement, the work goes through several phases. Depending on the type of study, a typical project starts with defining the problem and its expected outcomes and developing a work plan. It continues with each team member collecting the information necessary to analyze a particular question. Finally, the team draws on the information collected and provides recommendations for action. Increasingly, consultants (particularly those who provide IT services) are also getting involved in nuts-and-bolts implementation work, which may be done either as a follow-up project or as part of the original project. In other words, they roll up their sleeves and do the actual work they recommended to the client.

TEAM STRUCTURE

A consulting engagement is generally handled by a team, which can vary in size from two people (or in some cases, one consultant plus members from the client organization) to hundreds. The size of a project team will depend on the nature of the work and the philosophy of the firm. Many strategy-oriented firms staff teams with five or six people drawn from different levels of the organization. In contrast, IT projects may have dozens of people working on developing and implementing a new software system. As you might imagine, the bulk of the programming and design work for such projects is handled by junior employees, who bill out at lower rates. You may be able to get a feel for how a firm staffs its projects by comparing its revenues with the number of professionals—a high revenue per consultant generally indicates a high percentage of senior-level staff.

CLIENT INTERACTION

A critical part of any consultant's work is his or her interactions with the client. More and more these days, consulting firms are attempting to integrate client staff into project teams, though different firms have different ways of doing so. Many firms rely on client staff to help in project definition, research, and implementation. Particularly in the case of reengineering projects, the consultant often trains client staff members in new processes, new technologies, and/or new ways of thinking about their business.

Insiders report that while they typically enjoy executive-level support for their initiatives, they often encounter more resistance in their efforts from rank-and-file staff. This is where consultants' winning interpersonal skills come into play; consulting recruiters aren't just looking for people who can dazzle CEOs with their blinding insights—they're looking for consultants who can get along well with all levels of employees. After all, a critical component of the job is collecting and analyzing data that isn't always easy to come by. Those who excel at the job are those who can build relationships throughout the organizations they serve.

Key Jobs

As each firm has its favorite buzzwords, it also has unique terminology for its rank and file. While the titles might vary from firm to firm, the roles can basically be divided up as follows: analyst (also called research associate or staff consultant at some firms), consultant (or senior consultant), manager, and partner or VP. In addition, larger consulting firms hire a cadre of highly capable non-consultant staff into administrative and support positions. This is not a bad place to be if you've got skills in PowerPoint and you like to create slides.

ADMINISTRATIVE ASSISTANT

Most consulting firms have a fairly large pool of college-educated administrative assistants and support staff so that the consultants can keep focused on tasks that justify their $200-plus-per-hour billing rates. In addition to performing standard support functions, many have specific roles (recruiting, office administration, or website maintenance, e.g.). Most firms also have a group of graphic designers on staff to prepare materials for presentations.

ANALYST/BUSINESS ANALYST/SYSTEMS ANALYST/ PROGRAMMER ANALYST/RESEARCH ASSOCIATE/STAFF CONSULTANT/ASSOCIATE CONSULTANT

This is the position at the bottom of the professional pyramid. The vast bulk of analysts are young, talented, hungry, relatively recent college graduates. Many strategy consulting firms structure this position to last for two to three years, after which the analyst is expected to move on—perhaps to graduate school or another employer. This approach is less prevalent among IT consulting firms and other practices that specialize in operations or process consulting. In these areas, though some analysts do attend graduate school after a few years, it's more common to progress up the management ladder without leaving the firm to attend graduate school. The work itself—as well as the hours—can be quite demanding at the analyst level. It often includes field research, data analysis, customer and competitor interviews, client meetings, and (for IT consultants) heavy-duty programming.

ASSOCIATE/CONSULTANT/SENIOR CONSULTANT

Within strategy firms, this is the typical port of entry for newly minted MBAs (and increasingly for non-MBA graduate students). Senior consultants often perform research and analysis, formulate recommendations, and present findings to the client. Oh, and at many firms, they have to implement those great ideas, too. At the associate level, consultants start to practice their people-management skills, often taking responsibility for overseeing the work of junior consultants. Although this is usually a tenure-track position, a fair number of consultants will leave the advisory side business after two or three years to pursue entrepreneurial or industry positions.

MANAGER/ENGAGEMENT MANAGER/PROJECT LEADER/ ASSOCIATE PRINCIPAL

After a few years, a senior consultant will move up to manager (or an equivalent role to which it assigns a slightly different title). Regardless of the firm-specific nomenclature, the next rung on the ladder usually involves leading a team of consultants and analysts toward project completion, managing day-to-day project activities, providing thought leadership, and assuming primary accountability for project results. Some firms may hire MBAs with significant work experience directly into the manager position, particularly in their IT practices. In addition to having more rigorous responsibilities for managing the project team, the manager will typically act as the primary point person for client interactions.

VICE PRESIDENT/OFFICER/PRINCIPAL

Having mastered both the analytics and the people-management components of the job, consultants at this level are expected to be adept relationship builders within the firm and with clients. At this stage, consultants spend more time overseeing the overall quality of the services provided to the client, and relatively less time onsite with the rest of the project team. They also spend a greater proportion of their time providing thought leadership, developing analytical tools, and (oftentimes) determining internal administrative policies.

SENIOR VICE PRESIDENT/PARTNER/DIRECTOR

Congratulations! You've forded the River Jordan of consulting and arrived at the Promised Land. Note that some firms further subdivide partners into junior- and senior-grade. And, if you aspire to it, there's always that chairman or CEO position. Partners help determine the overall strategy and direction of the consulting firm, often leading new business development efforts in entire sectors and selling additional engagements to new and existing clients. Fortunately, as with other big-ticket sales jobs, the pay can be quite rewarding.

Real People Profiles

HEALTH CARE CONSULTING MANAGER

Age: 28

Years in business: 5

Education: BA in economics, Harvard University

Size of company: 60 employees

Hours per week: 50–60

Certification: none

Annual salary: $110,000 base salary, plus a performance-related bonus

How did you get your job?

I initially made contact through an alumnus from my college. The position that I eventually interviewed for was a perfect fit with my undergraduate focus—economics, with lots of coursework in health care, health care policy, and related extracurricular activities.

What are your career aspirations?

Eventually, I'd like to assume a business development role for a biotechnology or pharmaceutical company, and then progress toward a senior management position within the same (or similar) company.

What kinds of people do well in this business?

Clearly, an interest in health and healing the human body is important. You should have not only an interest in the business side of things, but also an interest in the science side. Without a good combination of knowledge and interest in both, you'll have a much harder time succeeding. You have to be commercially savvy and understand the many different forces acting on the health care value chain.

At my company, people generally come in with a business or science background and have to pick up whatever side they don't know to get ahead. Ultimately, our clients look to us to translate our knowledge and research findings into viable research strategies. As with traditional management consulting, you need to be a people person because the job requires a lot of working in groups and interfacing with clients. Presentation skills are also important.

What do you really like about your job?

In my position, I am surrounded by incredibly bright and dedicated people, which really does make my work more enjoyable. Also, for each project, the challenges that we have to address are almost always different, so we are all constantly learning about new issues and/or new therapeutic areas; it's hard to get bored here. Finally, you enjoy the opportunity to have a huge impact on clients' organizations—you're given a level of freedom and responsibility well beyond most people your age in other jobs.

What do you dislike?

In consulting, you're always at the beck and call of the client; consulting is a service industry, and firms will not maintain robust client relationships unless the consultants are constantly bending over backwards to answer their clients' requests. There are always clients that impose unrealistic timelines on projects that are difficult to manage. Also, consultants are always under pressure to be billable; this reality limits projects to issues that are of interest to (and paid for by) our clients, which leaves little or no time for academic or creative pursuits.

What is the biggest misconception about this job?

There are a few. One misconception surrounding the consulting profession in general is that the work is all high-level analysis for CEOs. Sometimes, the focus on building long-term, collaborative relationships means that part of your job involves doing outsourced work that the client can't handle due to resource constraints.

For health care consulting in particular, one popular misconception is that all we do is help pharmaceutical companies make more money. Ultimately, companies in a capitalist society do want to make a profit; however, health care consultants also help organizations bring innovative (and often lifesaving) technologies to market.

How can someone get a job like yours?

If you're a student, make sure to do something that suggests not just an interest in consulting, but an interest in health care specifically. Start a club. Take a leadership role in a health care group. Whether you're a student or an experienced professional, make sure to network and make contacts in the industry. The health care consulting industry is actually surprisingly small, and people at one firm tend to know people at other firms. Because of this, networking is the most effective way to get a job in this industry, since it saves you (and the employer) time and gives you a trusted resource to learn about the industry and the particular company.

The other advice I'd give to anyone looking to go into this business is to dismiss the idea that only the big consulting companies have health care practices; the majority of consultants in this category work for smaller firms that focus solely on health care. There are a ton of them out there, so broaden your search beyond the firms that are household names.

Describe a typical day.

There's really no typical day, but here's an example:

8:00 a.m.   I'm usually at work by 8 a.m. I spend a few minutes responding to overnight emails. Then I meet with my teams to see how they've progressed on the previous day's work. I probably manage four or five projects on any given day. Obviously, some of them are for external clients, but some are also for internal clients—other business units within my firm.

9:00 a.m.   I'm on a conference call with a client about one of my several ongoing projects. Depending on the stage the project is in, a typical conference call might involve speaking with the client to understand specific needs, or it might involve developing work plans that will address those needs. In this case, we've arranged a conference call to update the client on our progress on one of our projects, explaining the most significant findings from our research and one or two major problems that we've encountered along the way. The call lasts about three hours.

12:00 p.m.   I grab a quick lunch and eat it at my desk.

12:30 p.m.   The afternoon and early evening are spent both meeting with my teams to give them more direction on current projects and working on various product forecasting models that will ultimately be used by the client to make licensing or acquisition decisions. The afternoon is interspersed with multiple phone calls from clients, many of which will be fire drills—small requests, projects, or questions that need to be addressed immediately.

7:30 p.m.   On a day like this, I'm usually out of the office by 7:30 p.m.

SENIOR HR CONSULTANT

Age: 29

Years in business: 6

Education: BS in management, University of Michigan

Size of company: 16,000

Hours per week: Usually ranges from 45 to 55, more during weeks where I have a big client deliverable due. We're allowed an hour for lunch, but I usually eat at my desk and work through lunch.

Salary: $70,000 base

How did you get your job?

Before I worked at this firm, I worked in HR at a large, global natural resources company. I was only there for a year when I started looking outside the company. I did a lot of research on my own, and conducted a number of informational interviews. During one of these interviews, someone told me that HR consulting would be more interesting than working in HR for a company because I would work with a variety of different organizations on different projects rather than doing a lot of HR administrative work. So I eventually submitted my resume through the company's online process, and after three rounds of interviews, I was offered an entry-level analyst role. I've been here for about five years, and now specialize in helping companies develop reward and recognition programs.

What are your career aspirations?

At the moment, my primary career goal is to really develop my managerial capabilities—both in terms of client management and internal team management. That's the thing about moving up the ranks in consulting: When you start out, you have to develop strong project management and time management skills, but if you want to keep getting promoted, it's important to develop people management skills as well. For me, that's the part of the job where I've had the steepest learning curve. I really have to be adept at managing both downward (since I'm managing the more junior members of the team) and upward (since I'm the primary contact person for the senior team members) in my current role as a senior consultant.

What kinds of people do well in this business?

You have to have strong selling skills. In consulting, you are selling a service based on the organization's needs. The client has brought you in to provide advice on something. They have a problem they want fixed, whereas in internal HR you tend to be selling a concept or a change that the business may or may not perceive as necessary or timely or in their best interest. So you definitely need persuasion and negotiating skills. You also need to be intuitive and perceptive and have a really strong ability to ask the right questions. Finally, to be an effective consultant, you have to develop the ability to understand clients' problems, which may or may not have their roots in HR. For example, the client might think its compensation structure needs fixing, but in reality that can be a symptom of an underlying issue that is quite different. One of your roles as a consultant is to go in and talk to the client so you can root out these underlying issues rather than just jump in with a solution.

What do you really like about your job?

I like the variety of projects you work on in HR—in terms of the substance of the work, HR touches on so many different issues. On any given engagement, we might work on everything from helping a client launch its corporate values, implement a reward and recognition program for store employees, reassess its performance management system for top executives, or redesign job roles and job descriptions within the organization. The projects are very diverse, and you really use a range of skills, too. There's a heavy analytical component to the job, but relationship-building aptitude is also key. I feel like I really use both sides of my brain. And I love that I'm constantly learning; in HR consulting, you're always learning about people—what motivates them, what drives them to exceptional performance, how people can be managed more effectively to help the organization achieve its goals. It can really be fascinating work.

What do you dislike?

As an HR consultant, you're providing a service to an internal service provider, because HR is almost always viewed purely as a support function within a company. In other words, in this business, you feel as though you're pretty low on the corporate food chain. Even though some of the work can be strategic, there are times when it can be very, very operational. In terms of compensation, I'm definitely paid less than I would be if I worked for a strategy firm, and that occasionally bothers me. The worst thing, though, is that we're often hired to do the client's dirty work. Occasionally our recommendations involve layoffs, and that's not a particularly enjoyable part of the job.

What is the biggest misconception about this job?

Most people hear "HR" and they think compensation and benefits, or they think of recruiting—they think those are the only issues involved in HR, so they think that HR consulting isn't as analytical and strategic as other types of consulting. Most people don't realize the breadth of the organizational issues we tackle—everything from figuring out whether there are too many layers of management in an organization, to whether a company has an effective leadership development program in place, to designing an employment branding strategy so that a company can rebuild its reputation on campuses. Many of the issues we deal with are fairly strategic and have a significant impact on the organization. There's a common perception that HR departments are made up of paper pushers and that we just step in to help them push more paper.

How can someone get a job like yours?

Networking definitely helps. This isn't the kind of job where you necessarily come in right out of undergrad and work your way up—there are a lot of lateral hires who come in from internal HR roles and things like that. Basically, you have to know what you want to do and then make the effort to talk to people who work for the companies—and in the specific areas—that you're interested in. I really don't believe you can prepare yourself for the interviews (and for the job) without talking to people.

Describe a typical day.

8:00 a.m. I usually arrive at the office on the early side, and begin my day by checking email and voicemail. The messages in my inbox tend to determine the kind of morning I'm going to have. Sometimes I spend the first hour or hour and a half just being reactive—replying to internal and external messages or requests. If it's a quiet morning, I try to use the time to do any independent research or writing that's on my plate.

9:00 a.m. I dive into project-specific research. Right now, I'm on a project in which we're helping the client assess the effectiveness of the compensation practices for its sales force.

10:30 a.m. I meet with my case team to discuss how the project is going so far. This project is in its earliest stages, so as a team, we're doing the background work necessary to determine the best ways to tackle the client's question. At this meeting, I end up being the most senior consultant there because the project manager is out of the office.

12:00 p.m. I take about 35 minutes to pick up a sandwich and eat at my desk. For the rest of the hour, I'm organizing my thoughts on the morning meeting so that I can get back to the senior team members and apprise them of our progress.

1:00 p.m. Back in my office, poring through the preliminary benchmarking data that the junior team members have collected. I spend some time synthesizing the information into some top-level bullet points that will shape the rest of the analysis. During this time, I'm constantly interrupted by internal and external voice mail, answering questions.

4:00 p.m. I take a coffee break with one of the junior consultants who's just joined the firm. We have a formal mentor program in the office, and consultants are supposed to meet with their mentors once a month. She's just been assigned to her first project team, and so we catch up on her impressions so far.

4:30 p.m. I'm back at my desk, continuing to plow through data and the analysts' preliminary analysis. Based on this information, I'm developing a rough outline of action steps for the next phase of the project.

6:00 p.m.   Because the primary project I'm working on is in its early stages and I don't have a deliverable to produce, I probably won't have too many late nights this week. Before I leave, I always make a checklist of the things I need to work on the following day. If there's data I need to request either internally or externally, I'll put in a few calls and leave voicemails before I leave.

IT SYSTEMS ANALYST

Age: 23

Years in business: 1

Education: BA, interdisciplinary major in cognitive science, University of Virginia

Size of company: 8,000 employees

Hours per week: 48–52

Certification: none

Annual salary: $35,000

How did you get your job?

At my company, all recruiting is conducted via job postings on the website. During my senior year in college, I submitted 30-plus resumes to various companies, including the one that I'm currently working for. I was fortunate that my roommate's brother also worked at the company, and I think it helped that he was able to put in a good word for me.

What are your career aspirations?

In the short term, I'm focusing on moving up within this company. I've already received two promotions in the year since I was hired, and since the company is growing and adding new clients to its roster, I'm hoping there will be other chances to move up within my department. Beyond that, I'm not sure. From what I've experienced, it seems as though people in the industry move around a lot. We have a fairly high turnover rate among the analysts. You rarely find someone in the group who has been there longer than four years. Most people move to similar roles in other companies.

What kinds of people do well in this business?

Highly motivated, goal-oriented people tend to do well here. Personally, I dislike leaving any problem unsolved, which has served me well so far in this line of business. One of our main goals is to work around obstacles and resolve any issues in the most optimal way. Basically, you have to enjoy solving problems. And it also helps to be fairly extroverted and sociable, because there's a lot of interaction with other people—you have to be able to get along with your colleagues and team members. As you become more senior and have more client interaction and responsibility, you have to be able to win their confidence, too.

What do you really like about your job?

I like that I'm continually learning new things—coming straight out of undergrad, I had no idea what it was like to work within a large company like this one. I had no experience in college with this type of business, but many of the skills I gained from taking computer and cognitive science courses fit nicely within the systems analyst role. I like that the work is challenging and keeps me on my toes. I enjoy working with my colleagues, too. There's a great team of people working here, and we're all working toward a common goal. Finally, there are a lot of opportunities for advancement—the skills that I've learned working here will be transferable to other companies within and outside of this line of business.

What do you dislike?

First, I think the compensation is below market—for my job in particular, many people put in a lot of long hours and do not feel that they are compensated properly for the hard work they do. If you take a look at the amount that our account managers charge the client for an hour of a systems analyst's work, you can see there's a discrepancy. I get paid $17 an hour, but we charge the client $100–300 an hour depending on the assignment.

Also, there are a lot of inflexible rules and processes in this business. As an analyst, there are various standardized processes that we have to follow. Our managers like to create flow charts and organizational charts to demonstrate how things are done. Sometimes I think that all they do is sit around and restructure flow charts.

What is the biggest misconception about this job?

That it's always our fault if something goes wrong. Our group (the implementation group) has a lot of responsibility as analysts, and we accept that. However, just because we build the system doesn't mean that it's our fault if the client is unsatisfied with something. Our group seems to bear the brunt of criticism when things don't go right; more often that not, however, the system was set up properly, but it was the data (either provided by the client delivery team or the client themselves) that caused the issue.

How can someone get a job like yours?

The best way to get a job here is to go to the website and submit a cover letter and resume. It helps if you know a current employee or if you have some prior experience in systems design.

Describe a typical day.

7:00 a.m.   I typically get to work about two hours before any of my other coworkers. I like getting there that early in order to have some time of my own to work on projects without any distractions. I work best in the morning and find that I get most of my work done during this time. From about 7:00 a.m. to 8:00 a.m. I usually answer any email or voicemail that I received since the previous day. Then I map out what projects I will work on that day.

8:00 a.m.   Go to the break room and make myself a cup of tea.

8:10 a.m.   I resume working on projects from the previous day. I am working on updating specifications to be sent to programmers, testing programs (webs or interfaces), or creating reports (depending on what the need is). By 9:00 a.m., all of my other co-workers have arrived. By this time, I've already had two hours to get a jumpstart on the day's work.

9:00 a.m.   I find out what other analysts are working on, whether they have any time available to check the work that I've been doing, and whether they will have any work that I will need to check for them.

9:15 a.m.   I go back to working on my projects. Throughout the day I am constantly checking my email to see whether there are any ad hoc requests from the service center that I need to take care of. I am also looking for new meeting requests and email from the client suggesting system and plan design changes.

10:00 a.m.   Depending on the day of the week, we might have a client conference call. During the call, we'll go over any outstanding issues/projects or client concerns. After that, it's back to work on the day's projects.

12:00 p.m.   Most of the time I don't take a full hour for lunch. I always have plenty of work to keep me busy.

12:45 p.m.   Back to work on the day's projects and also to answer any email or voicemail that came in during my lunch break.

2:00 p.m.   Internal status meeting within our client team to see how our work is coming along and to plan out what needs to get accomplished to meet our deliverable schedule.

3:00 p.m.   After the meeting, I get back to the day's projects.

4:00 p.m.   Things are winding down now; either the final hour takes forever to pass, or I get a ton of work sent my way all at once and I rush to get as much of it done as possible before 5:00 p.m.

5:00 p.m.   If I'm lucky, I leave at 5:00. But if there are deliverables that need to be generated, then I'm there working as long as it takes to get things done. That sometimes means staying until 8 p.m. Otherwise, I try hard to get out of the office by 6 p.m. It's a personal thing, but I hate to carry work over to the next day. I like to get all things done that I set out to do at the beginning of each day. Because of this, my typical workday can last nine to twelve hours (much more than other analysts who tend to stick by the eight- to nine-hour workday).

The Workplace

Lifestyle

Hours and Travel

Diversity

Vacation

Compensation

Career Path

Insider Scoop

Lifestyle

The consulting lifestyle is known for being arduous. It is also relatively fast-paced, with consultants jetting around the country to client sites and working from deadline to deadline to gather lots of data to provide a client with a solid recommendation for action. As a consultant, you can expect to eat out a lot, almost never get home early, and rack up plenty of frequent flier miles. Major partying (and doing laundry, paying bills, shopping, and socializing) will usually have to wait until the weekend. Beware: It can be a difficult way to live. "I do not find it to be a sustainable lifestyle," says one insider. "There are people who I'm sure can sustain it, but, all in all, it's hard. It's the hours, but even more than that, it's the intensity; it's the travel. Even when you aren't at work, you still know you could be getting that voicemail at night."

When choosing a firm, make sure you like the people. The demands of the consulting lifestyle can be hard to take if you don't get along well with the people you're working with. One of the reasons why firms put so much stress on "fit" is because when you work long hours, often under the pressure of deadlines, collegial relationships (and working with team players) can make or break a case—and a consultant.

Hours and Travel

On the average, most consultants with strategy consulting firms work 55 to 60 hours in a typical week. Within the HR and IT consulting sectors, these numbers tend to be slightly lower, with most insiders reporting average work weeks in the 45- to 55-hour range. Health care consultants landed on all points in the spectrum, depending on whether they specialized on strategy or operations consulting. However, everyone will tell you there is no typical week. Before a presentation or a deadline, you may need to put in 80, 90, or even 100 hours, possibly including an all-nighter or two. In contrast, the time between projects, or during liberally staffed projects, may be relatively slow. Even so, consulting is not a nine-to-five job. Hours vary somewhat by firm, by office, and by practice, so you'll want to ask about hours before accepting an offer.

Consultants travel often and for days at a time. Although firms vary in their emphasis on the need to be at the client site, the primary factors affecting the amount of travel are the location of the client and the type of project. Consultants at some firms (such as Hewitt, an HR consulting firm) report that they travel significantly less than their counterparts at other firms. On average, a new undergrad or MBA hire can expect to be on the road at least two days a week. During a project, however, it is not uncommon to spend four days at the client site, week after week.

Diversity

Consulting firms look a lot like the schools where they recruit. There's not a lot of diversity. Like the brochures of those colleges and universities, the recruiting material tells a different story than that which is really taking place. Nevertheless, firms are increasingly trying to diversify their ranks. When you apply to a firm, you might want to ask about its diversity recruiting efforts and its success in retaining minority talent. Some minority and female professionals may be discouraged by the dearth of minorities and women in the manager-level ranks and above.

Insiders report that this is especially relevant in IT consulting, where the workforce "is mostly male and mostly white." In fact, experts estimate that women make up only about a quarter of the IT workforce. On the flip side, insiders report that there are more women in senior management roles at HR consulting (perhaps not entirely surprising, given that internal HR departments also have a reputation for attracting more women than men). Make sure that you're comfortable at the firm and that there's room for you to rise. It's worth inquiring about minorities and women in management positions: introducing yourself to them, discussing your career goals and how supportive the firm will be as you move toward them.

Vacation

Most firms offer new employees about three weeks of vacation per year, though it might be hard to take much of that time off mid-project. Project breaks provide a good opportunity to get away, and one big perk is that you'll have enough frequent-flier miles to travel anywhere in the world (provided you ever feel like flying again). Even if you don't take a formal vacation, most firms discourage a nine-to-five mentality. As a result, insiders report that you can often take a day or two off after a particularly grueling period.

Compensation

The major consulting firms are among the best-paying employers for new graduates. They are also known for offering excellent perks and benefits, such as annual off-site meetings at posh resorts and reimbursements of school expenses. Compensation in the industry rose dramatically through the 1990s, but it leveled off after 2001. At strategy firms, salaries were flat in 2002 and 2003, and began to rise in 2004. According to WetFeet research, in 2005, the average starting salary for a newly minted MBA going into consulting was $101,325—with a signing bonus of around $14,000.

Industry insiders expect that consulting compensation will continue to grow in coming years. As the economy improves and the war for talent intensifies among top firms, employers are likely to take more aggressive steps—including bumping up pay packages—to retain top-performing consultants. However, don't expect pay packages to increase at the same rate across consulting sectors; strategy consulting salary increases will outpace those of operations, HR, and IT consulting. Long term, the trend is for compensation from base salary to shrink, with increasing variable pay, such as year-end bonuses and other performance-based rewards.

Salaries and bonus packages at the top firms are generally within close range of each other, since these firms usually compete for the same pool of candidates. At the margins, there are slight differences in compensation: Lesser-known firms may offer slightly higher salaries or bonuses to attract top candidates, and some organizations have different ways of splitting up the bonus pie (for instance, linking a portion of the bonus to the firm's annual performance). To get more specific information on compensation practices, check out WetFeet's individual company Insider Guides.

UNDERGRADS

In the 2006–07 recruiting season, we estimate that the elite firms will offer starting salaries in the range of $55,000 to $70,000. Again, signing bonuses are not awarded across the board the way they once were, and can range up to $10,000. Undergrads joining a large IT services firm will likely be in the $40,000 to $55,000 range to start.

MBAS

In 2006–07, we estimate that MBAs hired into elite firms will start somewhere in the range of $100,000 to $130,000 for the top strategy firms. There's less of an emphasis on signing bonuses than in the past; these can run up to $30,000. Although consultants often have higher base salaries than investment bankers, bankers stand to make lots more—as much as 100 percent of their base—in their year-end bonuses. That's why some junior partners on Wall Street make more money than senior partners at consulting firms.

EXPERIENCED HIRES

Among the consulting firms that hire significant numbers of undergraduates, MBAs, and other advanced-degree candidates, compensation packages (including starting salaries, signing and relocation bonuses, and year-end bonuses) are fairly transparent. They also tend to be fairly consistent from one firm to the next: An entry-level consultant at Deloitte and an entry-level consultant at Accenture, for example, aren't likely to earn widely disparate salaries. Smaller, more specialized firms typically pay less than the larger firms, but it depends on the firm and the role you're hired into. In addition, the more junior you are, the less your total compensation will fluctuate due to vagaries in the economy or the performance of the individual firm in a given year.

For mid-career hires, compensation is considerably harder to predict. Consulting firms typically don't publicize details regarding the magnitude or the breakdown of the compensation packages they award to mid- and senior-level consultants. In the rare instances where mean or median compensation is reported for this segment of the consulting population, it's important to remember that there's considerably more variability around these averages than you'll see among the junior consulting ranks. As consultants move up the career ladder, the ratio of variable, performance-based pay to overall compensation tends to increase, while the ratio of base salary tends to decrease by a commensurate amount. Because experienced hires typically join consulting firms at a more senior level, compensation from one consultant to the next—and from one year to the next—tends to vary a great deal, depending on individual, group, and firm performance. For these reasons, compensation figures for mid-career hires aren't as readily available as salary information for consultants recruited directly from college campuses or MBA programs.

However, keep in mind that if you're coming into a highly specialized consulting practice with a few years of directly relevant work experience under your belt, there's probably more room for negotiation than there is for inexperienced hires (particularly if your specific skill set and professional background are hard to come by).

Below are the results of a couple of salary surveys available on CareerJournal.com.

Position	Average annual total compensation ($)*	
	2005	2004
Senior partner	317,339	267,300
Junior partner	191,664	166,000
Senior consultant	123,305	112,300
Management consultant	89,116	83,800
Entry-level consultant	65,066	63,100
Research associate	52,482	49,000

* Includes base salary, bonus and profit sharing.
Source: "Operating Ratios for Management Consulting Firms—2005 U.S. Edition,"
"Operating Ratios for Management Consulting Firms—2004 U.S. Edition,"
Association of Management Consulting Firms, New York, N.Y.

Position	Median annual base salary ($)*	
	2005	2004
Partner/vice president	200,000	170,000
Associate partner/principal/director	150,000	136,000
Senior manager	120,000	110,000
Manager/project leader	100,000	95,000
Senior/experienced consultant	85,000	85,000
Consultant/recent M.B.A.	70,000	65,000

* Includes approximately 240 respondents in 2005 and approximately 270 in 2004.
Source: "Compensation and Benefits in Management Consulting 2006,"
"Compensation and Benefits in Management Consulting 2005,"
Kennedy Information Inc., Peterborough, N.H.

Career Path

UNDERGRADUATES

Undergraduates generally join a consulting firm as analysts, although their titles vary. At many strategy firms, the analyst program lasts two to three years, after which you're encouraged to go to business school. This system, though, has been changing over the past several years. Firms have increasingly been promoting analysts into positions for which they traditionally hire MBAs, or into interim roles that fall between the undergraduate and MBA positions. If you choose to go to business school, many firms will pay your tuition, provided you return to the firm when you're done. At IT and HR firms, the hierarchy is a little more fluid; relatively fewer people leave after two or three years to pursue an MBA, and it's quite possible to move up the food chain without one.

MBAS

Consulting firms hire MBAs and other postgraduates right out of school or from industry. Most new MBA hires will come into a firm as associates; after two or three years they'll move to the next level, where they'll manage case teams. After managing projects for a couple of years, consultants may be promoted to principal, whereupon the focus shifts to more intensive client work and the selling of services. Finally, after six to eight years with a firm, a consultant might be promoted to partner. The benefits of partnership are big increases in salary and responsibility. The key function of partners at most firms is to cultivate clients and bring in new business.

ADVANCED-DEGREE CANDIDATES

Consulting firms often tap nontraditional candidate pools, including JDs, PhDs, and MDs. This is especially true for health care consulting practices; in fact, the majority of consultants in this field—unless they developed industry expertise working for a top-tier strategy consulting firm's health care practice—possess at least one advanced degree (and frequently more than one). HR consulting firms often hire people with advanced degrees in areas like industrial psychology or education. And many consulting firms are quite attracted to software engineers, process engineers and the like, depending on their area of focus.

If you are one of these candidates, find out which level you'll come in at—the same level as undergrads, MBAs, or experienced hires. Also, you should ask about the type of support you'll receive once you join the firm. Some organizations offer a mini-MBA training program, while others rely more heavily on mentorship and good old-fashioned on-the-job learning.

Insider Scoop

WHAT EMPLOYEES REALLY LIKE

Love My Job

Most people who work for consulting firms talk about how intellectually stimulating their work is. "The work is just phenomenal," one insider says. They enjoy the challenges of going into new settings and facing some of the most difficult issues business leaders have to deal with. Although most don't admit it openly, there's also a palpable excitement associated with being able to sit down with a CEO of a large firm and tell him or her what to do. Consultants also take pride in seeing the impact their advice has on clients' businesses.

People Power

The key resource of consulting firms, and some would say the only resource, is their people. All of the top-tier firms fill their offices by skimming the cream of the undergraduate and business school elite. Insiders tell us that working at a consulting firm is very much like being on a team with the best people from school: "People are invariably bright, interesting, hardworking, and motivated." (Sounds a little self-congratulatory, but it seems to be true.) Many insiders also say they enjoy socializing with their colleagues. A common refrain is, "These are people I'd be hanging out with anyway, even if we didn't work together."

Learning Environment

One of the thrills for many consultants is the constant learning that comes with the consulting workload. Whether you're learning about a new company or industry, talking to people in various parts of a client organization, or brainstorming ways to deal with challenging technical problems, consulting offers a steady diet of new cases and settings. "If our clients weren't dysfunctional, they wouldn't need us. There's definitely a unique satisfaction that comes from helping clients work through their most pressing challenges," reports one insider. Many consultants believe they wouldn't face such a wide variety of challenges in any other profession.

Pay and Perks

Very few consultants would publicly put it at the top of their lists, but most really like the pay and perks of the position. Even if you're not a particularly money-grubbing type, wouldn't you like to be able to afford a nice apartment, a new car, and to be able to pay off all those school loans in a couple of years? Moreover, many firms provide reimbursement of tuition expenses for some of their employees. Beyond that, all of the firms make sure that the extensive travel and the long hours are as painless as possible. Even if you don't relish the idea of staying in Phoenix for the next three months, you probably won't mind staying at the Phoenician Hotel.

Future Options

Many people enter consulting with the idea that they'll do it for a couple of years and then move on to something else. "It's hands-down the best job for someone [planning to start] a business or work at a Fortune 500 company. You can get behind the thought processes of key executives," says an insider. Although it may not be wise to give this top billing during your interview, a consulting firm is an excellent training ground, regardless of the type of work you ultimately wish to pursue, and many firms work hard to stay in touch with their alumni networks. Consulting gives people a chance to not only learn about different organizations and industries, but also a long list of contacts with whom they can network when they decide they're ready to move on.

WATCH OUT!

A Dog's Life

The travel, the hours, and the difficulty of maintaining a personal life top everyone's list of consulting complaints, regardless of the industry or function in which they specialize. One beleaguered IT consultant warns that "consulting firms care a lot about building relationships—just not your own." It's not that people in other professions don't work long, hard hours, but the consulting lifestyle, which often requires the consultant to be out of town four days a week for months at a time, is hard to maintain over the long run, especially for people with families. When we asked one of our insiders what kind of individual thrived as an IT consultant, problem-solving and technical savvy were not the first things he mentioned. "The ideal candidate would definitely be someone in their 20s, single, and with no kids. Otherwise, the job requires too much sacrifice." Some individuals actually thrive on the pace and excitement of the frenetic schedule. For many others, a few years are about all they want to put up with.

"I'd rather be . . ."

Consultants often express their desire to get into the thick of managing a company and start making management decisions. This may be partly a case of the grass being greener, but after giving advice to so many companies and executives, many consultants are eager to try their hand from the client side. They also complain about not getting the in-depth experience they'd get if they worked at a company. A large number of consultants leave after a few years to start their own businesses or work in operating companies.

What difference does it make?

Most people who go into consulting as a career say they do valuable, highly meaningful work. However, a common complaint among ex-consultants is that the work didn't seem as meaningful to them as they would have liked. As one says, "I felt like we did a lot of ephemeral strategy stuff for big companies that didn't really amount to much. I really didn't want to be working with conservative, old Fortune 500 companies. I wanted to be making a difference in a smaller setting, with real people."

Control

If the hours and the travel don't get to you, the unpredictability inherent in the consulting role just might. This is a complaint we've heard again and again from all consultants, regardless of function, industry, or (surprisingly) level of seniority. At the heart of consulting lies a service business, pure and simple; in a service business, the customer is calling the shots. "It's the one thing I just can't get over," says one insider at a top-tier consulting firm. "You just never know what you're going to get when you check your voicemail at 9 p.m. on a Tuesday. Everything can change on a moment's notice at the client's whim, and there's just nothing you can do about it."

No matter how good your advice, there's also no guarantee that a client will take it. If you like to see your ideas in action—or like to act on your ideas yourself—you may find a consulting gig frustrating. "At the end of the day, when all's said and done, you're telling somebody else what to do, and you don't have control over it," a consultant says. "You can sometimes feel like your hands are tied when you can't make that decision."

The Long Haul

By one insider's estimate, only one in ten people who start with a consulting firm is really a consultant at heart. As almost anyone who graduated from business school three years ago will tell you, very few classmates remain consultants for long. People leave for a variety of reasons, but most do leave. Therefore, if you're thinking that you'd like to set down roots and have something substantive to show for your work, you'll be better off in another type of organization.

Getting Hired

The Recruiting Process

There are two main routes into consulting. One goes directly from campus (undergrad and MBA, primarily) into entry-level positions (analyst or consultant). The other leads from industry into midlevel positions in specific practice groups (such as life sciences or health care), functions (like human resources), or technologies (CRM applications, for instance).

Of the consulting firms that actively recruit on campuses (and as we said before, not all of them do), most follow a fairly standard recruiting routine for undergraduate and graduate students. The typical tryout starts with an on-campus interview or two and finishes up with a day at the office where you want to work. Interviews can be one-on-one or two-on-one and usually include a basic resume review and a lot of questions designed to determine your fit with the organization. In addition, many interviews include every consulting recruiter's favorite fear-inspiring tool: the case interview.

Firms will be hiring in 2006–07. Recruiting will be competitive. If you're serious about a consulting career, know the firms before you talk to them, develop relationships with as many people at each firm as possible, and make sure you get the details right, from proofreading each correspondence to dressing sharply and appropriately for your interviews. And have your story down: Know why you want to be a consultant as well as why you want to be a consultant at [insert name of firm here].

"You need to think about whether this is the right job for you," an insider says. "You need to look at the people you meet as you're going through, and decide whether the firms you're interviewing with are places you'd be happy. That usually comes down to the people. If you're not looking at one of the larger, established brand names, you've got to be clear about the firm's position, where its flow of consulting projects is going to come from. With the established firms, it's probably worth understanding how they've dealt with the last couple of years, how busy people have been, and [whether] the consultants been given sufficient experience."

"You can't go half-hearted," another insider says. "For people who are nontraditional types of hires, especially humanities majors, find out which companies typically hire people like you. If you're a businessperson with a stunning GPA, it's not guaranteed that you'll get interviews. If you have a GPA that isn't spectacular, you'll have to think of other ways to get that interview." Expect the bar to be high.

Consulting Interview Breakdown

A typical consulting interview generally consists of several parts. At a minimum, these include an introductory "get to know you" conversation, a resume review, a Q&A section designed to enable you to prove that you're qualified for the job, a few behavioral questions, a case interview question, and a follow-up discussion that asks what *you* want to know about *them*. Although the case interview portion often inspires the most terror, the other portions of the meeting are every bit as important. In fact, many HR and IT consulting firms don't even use case interviews, opting instead for a purely resume-based and behavioral interviewing approach. Regardless of that particular interviewer's approach—and of the type of consulting firm with which you're interviewing—the qualities that she is looking for will be fairly standard across the board. The attributes your consulting interviewer is seeking include the following:

• High energy and enthusiasm

• Team orientation

• Analytical skills

• Problem-solving ability

- Intellectual curiosity

- Excitement about consulting

- Knowledge about what makes the interviewing firm different

- Ability to pass the airplane test—do they really want to sit next to you on a long overseas flight?

- Interpersonal skills

- Relevant industry/functional experience

Whether you're participating in a little get-to-know-you banter with your interviewer or clobbering your sixth consecutive case interview question, you should be cognizant of whether you're establishing that you possess these necessary skills. With that in mind, we've outlined the major categories of questions you're likely to encounter in a consulting interview.

RESUME-BASED QUESTIONS

We would have thought that this would go without saying, but according to our insiders, it doesn't, so we'll say it: Know your resume inside and out, and be prepared to speak intelligently about anything that appears on it. This includes taking a moment to consider why you chose your university, your course of study, and any extracurricular activities or personal interests that you've included on the one-page summary of your life. Many candidates gloss over these discussions, but your answers to resume-based questions say a lot about you.

As you prepare for your interviews, take a good hard look at your resume. Consider the points you'd most like to convey, and then make sure you're armed with two or three talking points about each item. If there's something particularly unusual on your resume (you ran the New York Marathon, you went to medical school before you completed

your MBA), be sure to practice your spiel. Once you know how you'll discuss each bullet point, take your preparation one step further: Think ahead about how each bullet
point on your resume can be turned into a compelling (but short) story that demon-
strates your aptitude for consulting.

BEHAVIORAL QUESTIONS

Though firms vary in the degree to which they rely on the case interview, almost every
consulting interview—regardless of whether it's with a strategy, HR, IT, or industry-
specific consulting firm—will involve some variation of the behavioral interview. In
behavioral interviews, candidates are asked to cite experiences—professional, academic,
and personal—in which they've actively demonstrated specific attributes. Examples of
behavioral questions include, "Tell me about a time you made a mistake," "Tell me
about a time when you had to solve a problem," or "Tell me about a time when you
found yourself wandering naked through the mountains of Tibet carrying only
matches, a compass, and a bar of chocolate. How did you react?"

Even though the questions may seem more Barbara Walters and less Larry King than
you'd expect, behavioral interviewing is based on the premise that patterns of past
behavior most accurately predict future performance. Advocates of behavioral interviewing report that this technique enables interviewers to most accurately assess whether a
candidate possesses the requisite skills and personality for on-the-job success. The logic
is appealing: Anyone can rattle off a list of attributes commonly sought by investment
banks, but successful candidates can readily substantiate these claims with examples
that *demonstrate* competence in any given area. For example, it's fairly easy for a candidate to claim exceptional problem-solving capabilities knowing that consultants assign
a great deal of importance to logical, results-focused thinking. In a behavioral interview, however, the interviewer might ask the candidate to describe a particular project—
completed during a summer job, perhaps, or in an academic context—that required a
great deal of problem-solving aptitude.

What does all of this mean for you, the job seeker? *It means that knowing the job for which you are applying and knowing exactly how your experiences and achievements relate to that job are the most important things you can do to prepare for consulting interviews.* You may be accustomed to preparing for interviews through a line-by-line audit of each individual bullet point on your resume. In some interviews, this is a sound approach. An interviewer may very well ask, "I see you worked at XYZ Corporation over the summer. What were your responsibilities there?" Questions like this will certainly arise in consulting interviews, but perhaps more prevalent are questions like, "Tell me about a time that you took on a responsibility that perhaps wasn't part of your official job description." You could choose to point out that at your previous job you designed a comprehensive training program for new employees, organized guest speakers, and designed metrics to track the program's efficacy. Alternatively, you might choose to highlight your involvement in a particular B-school study group, in which you took up the flag for an ailing team member and wrote a presentation that technically fell outside the scope of your assigned duties. Either example works, as long as it shows that you've taken initiative in the past.

STRESS INTERVIEWS

Picture the scene: A young man enters the interview room cautiously and, remembering all the advice he's heard, greets his interviewer politely and sits down only after he's asked to. His interviewer then proceeds to whip out a newspaper and immerse himself in it. One minute passes, five, ten. . . . The candidate remains posed anxiously on his chair, waiting for the interview to begin. Finally after 20 minutes, the interviewer folds up his paper, turns to the baffled, silent candidate and announces that the interview is over. "You're obviously not the type of person who would succeed at our firm."

Wait a minute! Does this sort of interview "Code Red" actually still happen? It certainly happens less frequently than it used to, but a few of our insiders (and thankfully, only a few) report that these sorts of tactics still very much come into play at a few firms.

Unfortunately, not only do these types of scenarios sometimes emerge at the whims of particularly bitter consultants who resent having to conduct interviews, but they're also occasionally sanctioned as part of the official interview process. "Stressful situations are just part of the job, so we have to assess whether a candidate can stay composed if confronted with stress," says one insider. Because most firms recognize that these kinds of tactics don't leave candidates with the most favorable impression of them, you won't encounter them frequently, but if you do, keep your wits about you. Stay polite, respectful, personable but assertive. A few moments of awkwardness won't disqualify you, but tears certainly will.

The Case Interview

In essence, the case interview is nothing more than a simplified business problem designed to serve as a platform for the interviewee to show off his or her problem-solving abilities. Think of it as the business equivalent of the Kevin Bacon game; there's a beginning and an end, and your interviewer wants to see if you can walk through it on the fly without any extraneous steps. It's also a little bit like fraternity hazing. Anyone sitting on the other side of the table has been through it and survived, and, as a result, believes it to be a legitimate means of separating the wheat from the chaff. So, like it or not, you've got to be able to crack the case when it's presented.

We summarize the case interview here, but for in-depth discussion, see WetFeet's best-selling *Ace Your Case!*® series of guides.

THE SETUP

The case question usually starts off as a brief description of a typical client problem: "I'm a medical device manufacturer, and my revenue is going down." This may be a simplified version of a project from the consultant's own background, or it may be something made up to draw on—or differ from—things on your own resume. In any case, the interviewer will typically provide a package of background information about the company, the industry, and the problem. The recruiter will end with, "What would you do now?"

THE PROCESS

As the applicant works through the answer, the recruiter will continue to provide more details about the case and ask a variety of questions to probe the candidate's thought process. During the course of the discussion, the interviewer might ask the applicant to explain the reasoning behind a particular approach. In other cases, the interviewer might play devil's advocate and challenge the candidate's assertions, or role-play as an unruly and uncooperative client.

WHAT IT MEANS

Although a few firms have bucked the trend by placing considerably less emphasis on the case interview ("Let's face it. Eighty percent of the students at the top schools won't have any problem with the analytics of the job," says one MBA assigned to a recruiting role), most continue to view the case interview as the primary means of determining a candidate's aptitude. The key is not to get the "right" answer, since usually there is no one right answer. Rather, the interviewer is hoping to get some insight into how the applicant thinks and solves problems. For better or worse, many recruiters also see the case question as the Rosetta stone to a person's character, intelligence, sense of humor, background, personal habits, and virtually anything else you want to throw in.

HOW TO ANSWER

Case interview success doesn't require the ability to shoot from the hip and solve a highly complex problem in the course of five minutes. Rather, it depends primarily on your thought process and presentation.

Interview Prep

The best way to prepare for a consulting interview is to go through a few practice sessions with a friend or a mock interviewer. This will give you invaluable experience in spinning out a quick, cogent, and poised response to a case question and make your unavoidable encounter with one in the interview room that much easier.

TIPS FOR SAILING THROUGH THE CASE INTERVIEW

1. Listen carefully to the material presented. Take notes if you want to, and be sure to ask questions if you are unsure about details.

2. Take your time. Nobody is expected to have a brilliant solution to a complex problem on the tip of his or her tongue. If you need a minute or two to collect your thoughts and work through your answer, say so.

3. Offer a general statement—or framework—up front to serve as an outline for your answer. Although the framework can be something as elaborate as a 3C (customer, company, competition) model, it can also be as simple as something like: "If you're asking about declining profits, then I'd want to check into factors affecting cost and factors affecting revenue. On the cost side…" As you proceed with your answer, draw on the outline of your framework.

4. Try to focus first on what you think are the key issues in the case. Many interviewers will be checking to see if you operate by the 80/20 rule, which means that you should first address the broader issues that will get you 80 percent of the way through a good solution.

5. Orient your answer toward action. Remember, the goal of a consulting gig is to provide the client with actionable recommendations.

6. Don't be afraid to think out loud. The interviewer is looking as much for evidence of a logical thought process as for a brilliant solution to the case problem.

7. Be conscious of resources. A lot of consulting work is figuring out how you're going to collect the information you need to answer a question—without costing the client a fortune. It's probably not a good idea to suggest interviewing dozens of CEOs to see how they have dealt with similar issues, because setting up those interviews would be a nightmare.

8. Present your answer with conviction. A consultant's success depends largely on his or her ability to convince clients to embark on difficult courses of action. How you present yourself plays a big role in this.

9. Have fun with the case! Consulting is really like a steady succession of case interview questions. If you are going to do well in consulting, you need to enjoy the intellectual challenge of analyzing tough problems and coming up with good answers on the fly.

Interviewing Tips

Although the top consulting firms hire hundreds of people every year, thousands and thousands of people compete for those positions. There's no surefire way to guarantee an offer, and there are few, if any, back doors into the organizations. In most cases, your best bet will be to go through the standard on-campus recruiting program and bid lots of points to get on those schedules. Beyond that, however, insiders tell us that there are a number of ways you can improve your chances in the interview process. Here are a few of their suggestions about how to prepare for your interviews:

1. Be ready to give a good answer to the question, "Why do you want to go into consulting?" Of course, there is no single right answer to this question, but there are wrong answers. The worst is to say something you don't really believe. Even if you do happen to slip it by the interviewer, you'll pay the price later.

2. Keep a high energy level. Recruiters get tired of asking the same questions, so it's up to you to inject some excitement into the interview. At the end of a long day in the cubicle, chances are good they'll remember more about your enthusiasm than about the bullet points on your resume.

3. If strategy consulting firms are on your short list, there's no way around the case interview. To get an offer from one of these elite consulting firms, you'll need to nail not only one, but as many as eight or ten different case questions during your three rounds of interviews. To do your best, insiders recommend that you attend any informational sessions about the case interview, do some case interview drills with a friend, sign up for mock interviews (if possible), and, of course, buy copies of the *Ace Your Case!*® series, WetFeet's best-selling consulting case interview prep guides.

4. Know what distinguishes the firm you're interviewing with from its competitors, and be able to explain why you want to work for them. Everybody knows that most people who want to go into consulting will interview with all the firms. However, you still need to demonstrate that you have enough interest in a particular employer to have done your homework.

Grilling Your Interviewer

In any interview, there comes a point where the tables are turned, and you're asked if there's anything you'd like to know from your interviewer. Not surprisingly, this is where many a candidate assumes he's done and lets his interview guard down. Of course, it would be unwise to abandon your interview persona (and we know you have one) at this stage, but nonetheless, the question remains: when it's your turn to ask the questions, what do you ask?

First of all, we should tell you that this is a topic on which reasonable people can (and do) disagree. Some insiders insist that you should always ask a question when offered the opportunity, and that your question should prove to your interviewer how much research you've done on the industry and the specific firm. We disagree. If the sole purpose of your question is to prove that you've checked out the firm's website, read its annual report, or read *Consultants News*, chances are your interviewer can tell a mile away.

Our advice on the issue is actually fairly straightforward: stick to those questions that you'd genuinely like answered, as well as questions that would be difficult for you to answer without the benefit of insider insight. If you really *do* want to know why your interviewers chose to work at Firm XYZ, then ask away, and don't worry that your interviewer will dismiss your question as a waste of time. We didn't speak to a single recruiter who dinged a candidate because their questions weren't insightful or penetrating enough. Of course, recruiters are quick to point out that your questions shouldn't display blatant ignorance regarding the industry, the company, or the specific position for which you're interviewing. You won't win points for playing it safe and asking your interviewer to describe the last project he worked on, but you probably won't lose any, either. If you've had a reasonably good interview so far (and perhaps even more so if you haven't), you may not want to rock the boat with questions designed to demonstrate how very clever you are.

If you're reading this and thinking that you couldn't possibly ask a plain vanilla question that doesn't dazzle your interviewer with the power of your blinding insight, don't worry! There are ways to jazz up your standard-issue "What Questions Do You Have For Us?" replies. One recruiter suggests that candidates re-frame relatively broad questions by personalizing them. For example, rather than asking your interviewer to describe the firm's culture, you may choose to put it this way: "I've talked to several consultants representing a range of practice areas, and a number of them have mentioned that they've been surprised by how accessible the senior people are at this firm. I wonder if this is consistent with what you've experienced, and whether you feel that this is indicative of the culture throughout the company." Provided that you actually have spoken to consultants (and don't even think about referring to fictitious conversations), this question allows you to establish your sincere interest in the firm while remaining relatively safe.

Another insider tip: Like your mother said, remember to be interested, not interesting. Pay attention when your interviewer introduces himself, and make a mental note of the geographic location and practice area or business unit he represents. When the spotlight turns to you, give your question a group-specific slant. For example, "You mentioned earlier that you specialize in rewards consulting. I'd be interested to learn more about how you arrived at this specialization, and whether your path is representative of the typical career progression here." Again, this question isn't so generic that your interviewer's eyes glaze over, but it doesn't suggest that your primary objective is proving your business acumen.

As long as you play by a few simple ground rules, insiders report that this really is just a chance for you to resolve any outstanding questions you have about the firm: issues that aren't necessarily apparent from the company's recruiting literature or website, or topics that weren't addressed in the company's information session. For example, you may want to ask about the company's official or unofficial mentoring programs; the criteria on which your performance will be assessed; how analysts' responsibilities typically evolve from their first year to the second; or the types of training programs (either orientation programs or ongoing job-related training) that would be available to you if you joined. Another insider tip: try to introduce your question with a little "tag" that explains to the interviewer why you're asking a particular question. For example, "One of the things I really found useful during my summer internship was the formal mentoring program that the company offered. I wonder if you could tell me about mentoring at your organization—do you have a formal program, or is informal mentoring more the norm?" Even if it's short and sweet, adding a personal touch will convince your interviewer that you're sincere in asking your question, rather than asking it just for the sake of asking it.

While you're crafting questions to lob at your interviewer, keep one last thing in mind: Most of your interviewers will be on a fairly tight timetable, and they'll be struggling to keep each interview to the 30- or 45-minute time slot it's been allotted. Learn to read your interviewer. If it's clear that she is trying desperately to wrap things up, don't feel pressured to ask your questions simply because you've prepared them. If you sense she's trying to move things along, a diplomatic response might be, "Thanks. I'm conscious of your time restraints and know that the interview schedule is tight. Perhaps I could take one of your cards and contact you later with any questions?" This way, you've left it up to her—if she's indeed at the end of her interview tether, she'll take you up on your offer. If she's got plenty of time, she'll invite you to ask away (and she'll be impressed that you've respected her schedule, which will win you extra points).

WHAT NOT TO DO

When it comes time to ask questions of your interviewer, there are a few sand traps that you should avoid like the plague. As one insider put it, "it's probably not a good idea to ask me anything that would make me question your intelligence or your integrity." In addition, you don't want to ask questions that display a blatant ignorance of the industry, the firm, or the nature of the job for which you are applying (i.e., probably not a great idea to ask your Deloitte interviewer what sets his firm apart from firms like PwC and KPMG: you can't afford to botch the details here).

Other types of questions to avoid include the following:

Presumptuous Questions

"I really want to work overseas at some point during my career. How can I improve my chances of being transferred to my first-choice office?" Well, let's see: You could start by *getting a job offer with this firm in the first place.* Interviewers typically dislike questions from candidates who prematurely assume they'll receive an offer, so be careful to avoid even the teensiest bit of presumptuousness in your questions.

Questions with a Tattle-Tale Tone

"I know that your company eliminated about 15 percent of its workforce back in 2001 and 2002. I'm curious whether your firm has developed a better way of adjusting hiring activity to the market." This is a question that you may indeed want to ask, but use your better judgment. After all, it's a little early in the process to reveal your cynicism about the industry.

Questions that Suggest You Have Underlying Concerns about the Job

"One of the things I've heard over and over again is that the travel is really exhausting and that you never sleep in your own bed. How many weeks out of the year would you say you're on the road?" Interviewers expect that by the time you've gotten to this stage in the process, you know what you're getting into and that you've accepted it. If you're still worried about evenings, weekends, and vacations, you're interviewing for the wrong job.

Questions that Indicate You've Already Got an Exit Strategy

"What do people typically do once they leave your firm? Are they able to find jobs with other consulting firms relatively easily?" Unless the company with which you're interviewing offers an analyst/associate position that is expressly described as a two- or three-year program (and this will not be the case for all firms), you should probably avoid giving your interviewer the impression that you've already got your sights set on bigger and better things.

For Your Reference

Consulting-Speak

General Consulting Information

Health Care Consulting Resources

HR Consulting Resources

Technology Consulting Resources

WetFeet Resources

Consulting Firm Websites

Consulting-Speak

To help prepare you for both your interviews and a possible career in the field, we've asked our insiders to give us the most up-to-date consulting jargon. Beware: Unauthorized use of these terms has been known to seriously offend every known species of consultant.

2x2. Pronounced "two by two," this is a favorite consulting tool used to analyze a number of items along two dimensions. It's basically a graph with X and Y axes that cross in the middle, creating four different sectors. Don't be surprised if you're asked to produce one of these during your interview.

Activity-based costing. Assigns overhead costs to customers and products based on the amount of activity and resources spent on these customers and products.

Back-of-the-envelope calculation. A rough, on-the-spot estimate. Among other things, the case interview (see below) is intended to test whether your comfortable performing calculations of this type.

Balanced scorecard. Enhances performance measurement by creating a "scorecard" based on a balance of four perspectives—customer, internal, financial, and future. Allows companies to measure both daily performance and long-term strategy.

Benchmark. Here's another standard-issue item from the consulting toolbox. Benchmarks are levels of performance or output against which one can evaluate the performance of another. A benchmark study is an analysis of the performance of companies along specified dimensions. For example, a software firm might hire a consulting firm to conduct a benchmark analysis of how much other firms are spending on customer service.

Big Four. In a consulting context, the Big Four generally refers to the consulting firms currently or formerly affiliated with the big four accounting firms—generally not to the accounting firms themselves. Just in case you got lost somewhere along the way, here's a quick re-cap: The Big Four were the Big Five until Andersen went bankrupt after the Enron scandal. By then, consulting firms were already separating from their audit partners: Ernst & Young had sold its consulting practice to Cap Gemini to form Cap Gemini Ernst & Young (now Capgemini) and KPMG Consulting had broken off from its accounting side and gone public (it has since changed its name to BearingPoint). Other members of this group include PricewaterhouseCoopers, which sold its consulting unit to IBM in July 2002, and Deloitte Consulting, where a buyout by consulting partners was scotched (the consulting arm has since been reintegrated into Deloitte). The Big Four firms offer strategic advice, information systems support, and other more specialized consulting services to many of the same corporations served by the elite consulting firms. They also boast strong information technology capabilities on projects requiring heavy systems implementation work, and in some cases offer outsourcing to compete with the technology and systems consulting firms.

Big picture. The larger, or overall perspective.

BPO (business process outsourcing). Business process outsourcing is the contracting of a specific business task, such as payroll, to a third-party service provider. Usually, BPO is implemented as a cost-saving measure for tasks that a company requires but does not depend upon to maintain their position in the marketplace.

BPRE (business process re-engineering). The process of analyzing, redefining, and redesigning business activities to eliminate or minimize activities that add cost and to maximize activities that add value. The term was coined in the early '90s, and it suggested that organizations start from a blank sheet, completely reconceptualize major business processes, and use information technology to obtain breakthrough improvements in performance. The term became unpopular in the late nineties and many business people associate BPR with failures.

BTO (business transformation outsourcing). Takes BPO a step further. Providers of BTO services claim that new types of outsourcing relationships can help initiate technology-based business transformations—rather than simply lowering costs.

Buy-in. Agreement from others. Usually refers to support for an initiative from a company's senior managers or executives. Also refers to support within a company for a project or initiative proposed by consultants.

Change management. Here's a $5 buzzword that sounds like it's making things clear, when really it's just muddying up an already fuzzy concept. Most firms use this term to refer to a specific type of consulting work dedicated to such things as helping a company restructure its organization and cope with the human problems that accompany such an effort.

CRM (customer relationship management). Communication technology that helps companies manage customer information. CRM systems are often tightly integrated networks that see movement in sales activity, predict product demand, and manage the logistics of complex teams to serve the buyer and seller.

Case team. Project team, usually composed of anywhere from two to fifteen consultants.

Core competencies. Things a company does best.

Cycle time reduction. Decreasing the time it takes to complete a business process.

Deliverables. The tangible output, product, result, or solution you give (i.e., deliver) to the client. If you promise an analysis of shipping costs, for instance, that's your deliverable. Deliverables typically come with dates (when you will deliver).

ERP (enterprise resource planning). An IT solution to streamline operations by connecting all parts of a business electronically—including HR, billing, and inventory. A popular consulting project during the '90s, ERP spurred double-digit annual growth for firms.

Engagement/project/case/study/job. These are all different ways in which the firms refer to a specific project. Interviewers often note which term you use—just to see whether you've read the company literature. Using the wrong word is not an automatic ding, but you'll impress your interviewer if you get it right.

End-to-end. A marketing term—particularly pervasive in IT consulting circles—that can mean a number of different things. Think of it as the IT consulting equivalent of "soup to nuts." It's almost always followed by the term "solution," which is an equally prevalent (and equally amorphous) term. Depending on the context, it can mean that the consulting firm offers advice on everything from strategy to implementation, product design to delivery, or all parts of a business (from the first element of the value chain to the last). Though the term has no formal scope and gets used for a lot of different things, you can interpret it to mean, "we do a lot of different things that relate to each other."

Framework. Basically, a framework is any kind of structure you can use to look at a problem. It can be as simple as, "The company's problems stem from both internal and external factors." Or it can be something more MBA-ish, like Porter's Five Forces. Consultants love frameworks, and the more you use them (up to a point), the more analytical you'll sound.

Functional area. One of the major functions performed in operating a business (e.g., marketing, finance or sales).

Implementation. These days, nobody admits to doing just pure strategy work. The reason? Too many consulting firms were criticized for leaving behind a big stack of slides that never resulted in any action by the client. As a result, all of the firms now talk about how they work with clients to make sure that their expensive analyses and recommendations are actually implemented.

Industry or Corporate America. Consultants' term for the companies that they serve (everyone besides a consultant or other advisor such an investment bank).

IT and IS. Abbreviations for information technology and information systems.

Lift and shift. Migrating an entire business function (i.e., the HR function) outside the company to a third-party provider (i.e., outsourcers).

Methodology. An analytical tool or approach used to solve a client's problem.

On the beach. In consulting, this refers to any period during which you aren't staffed to a project. Although you won't necessarily see any sunshine here, you also won't have to be any place in particular, so there's a chance you'll be able to leave the office early, do your laundry, pay your bills, and maybe even see your honey.

On-site. Working at the client's offices.

Operations. Refers to all of the day-to-day tasks associated with the running of a company. In a manufacturing company, this includes the buying and processing of raw materials as well as the sale and distribution of the final products. Many consulting firms do a big business providing operations advice. At the simplest level, this just means that they help clients run their businesses better.

Outsourcing. To reduce overhead expenses, lots of companies are turning to outsiders to provide many of the functions and services traditionally done in-house. Popular candidates for outsourcing include accounting services, marketing communications, payroll management, and data processing. Increasingly, public firms are turning to these services because they create stable revenue flows, which their investors like.

Pain point. Refers to a recurring business problem or challenge that inhibits an organization's ability to achieve its objectives. For example, a pain point for a pharmaceutical company may be navigating the regulatory environment in an effective manner. For most consulting hopefuls, the dreaded case interview would constitute a pain point.

Porter's Five Forces. Harvard Business School Professor Michael Porter's famous explanation of the five forces that drive industry competition: potential entrants, suppliers, substitutes, buyers, and competitors.

Presentation. In the traditional consulting project, the presentation was the means by which a consulting firm shared all of its insights and recommendations with a client company. The client's top management team would assemble in a boardroom, and a partner or case team manager would spin through dozens of overhead slides displaying all of the analysis his or her firm had completed. Although the standard overhead slide-show is now considered a bit sterile, it's still a popular drill at most firms.

Reengineering. Reengineering lost its cachet in the mid-'90s. In its purest sense, a reengineering project was supposed to involve a complete rethinking of a company's operations from ground zero.

Shareholder value analysis. The goal of many companies is to enhance their value to shareholders, and they engage lots of consulting firms to help them do it. There are all manner of ways, proprietary and not, to analyze shareholder value.

Stop the bleeding. Addressing a company's most urgent, serious and/or costly business issues first. Similarly, a company may be referred to as "hemorrhaging cash" or "bleeding talent."

Supply chain. The complete set of suppliers of goods and services required for a company to operate its business. For example, a manufacturer's supply chain may include providers of raw materials, components, custom-made parts and packaging materials. Supply chain management refers to the management of supplier relationships in order to gain competitive advantage in cost, service, and quality.

Systems integration. Assembling complete systems out of many components, and integrating them so they all work together.

Thought leadership. Refers to the process through which consulting firms preserve and institutionalize their intellectual capital. In much the same way that college professors are expected to both teach *and* publish, consulting firms are expected to both advise companies *and* think big thoughts. *Thought leadership* refers to a company's intellectual capital—it might refer to a tool or a framework used to solve a business problem that can be applied to other consulting engagements. A company's thought leadership content is often preserved internally, but firms routinely share their ideas and frameworks with the broader business community through white papers, journal articles, and other publications. BCG's growth-share matrix and Watson Wyatt's human capital index are examples of thought leadership; these consulting firms developed frameworks for solving business problems that are then shared with the broader business community.

Toolkit. A collection of methodologies or tools that consultants can use to help solve a problem.

Total quality management. Teaches that quality, like everything else, has an intrinsic value and is important to customers. Spreads customer orientation throughout the company; empowers employees to fix problems in order to sustain world-class quality of products, services, and processes. Sets goal of meeting rigorous quality standards; emphasizes continuous improvement.

True north. The place you want to get to. If you're heading true north, you're moving in the right direction.

Value chain analysis. An analysis of all of the processes that go into a product, from the gathering of raw materials needed to make the product to the delivery of the final product to the customer. At best, each stage adds value to the product.

Vertical. A vertical consulting practice is one that offers a general management consultancy applicable to one industry only (e.g., health care), whereas a horizontal consulting practice (like HR or IT) focuses on a specific discipline applicable to many different industries.

Virtual office/hoteling. Sexy terms for an office setup in which nobody has a personal desk or office. Means you could be hanging out with the clerks at Copymat.

White-space opportunity. A money-making opportunity in an area you aren't set up to make money in. Think of it as an unbridged gap between what you do and what others do, or an untapped source of growth.

General Consulting Information

A general resource for information about the consulting industry is *Consultants News*, published by Kennedy Information. For more information about this and other Kennedy publications, visit ConsultingCentral.com or the Kennedy Information website, www.kennedyinfo.com.

The Professional and Technical Consultants Association (PATCA) can be found at www.patca.org. At this site, you'll find links to PATCA's quarterly journal, with interesting articles on such topics as biotechnology and other technical consulting fields.

Reading *Fast Company, Fortune, Forbes, BusinessWeek, Business 2.0*, the *Wall Street Journal*, and the *New York Times* is an easy way to stay up-to-date on the latest events and issues that management consultants address, and will arm you with plenty of information for your interviews. Each of these publications has a corresponding website that's worth a visit.

If you're currently a student and your library offers access to Factiva (an online database that offers full-text articles from thousands of individual publications, including all of those listed above), you can search for industry-specific and company-specific news to prepare for interviews. Plunkett Research—another online database—also offers a wealth of information about the consulting industry, including detailed profiles of consulting firms, white papers that describe the trends shaping the industry, and industry-specific interview tips. If your campus library offers Plunkett Research Online—or if it offers the print versions of its consulting industry guide—it's worth taking a look at these resources in advance of your interviews. If you're pressed for time and need a quick-and-dirty synopsis of a particular firm, take a look at the Hoovers online database (www.hoovers.com).

Health Care Consulting Resources

ONLINE RESOURCES

ADVANCE for Health Information Professionals
(http://health-information.advanceweb.com)
News, vendor listings, and jobs for health information professionals.

BCBSHealthIssues.com (http://bcbshealthissues.com)
Published by the Blue Cross and Blue Shield Association, this site features news relating to public policy and health care insurance coverage.

Health Management Technology (www.healthmgttech.com)
Health care–IT management magazine.

HealthWeb (www.healthweb.org)
Database of health care websites.

Knowledge@Wharton Health Economics page
(http://knowledge.wharton.upenn.edu/index.cfm?fa=viewCat&CID=6)
Covering health care business and strategy issues.

Managed Care Magazine (www.managedcaremag.com)
A guide for managed care executives and physicians covering capitation, compensation, disease management, accreditation, contracting, ethics, practice management, formulary development, and other health insurance issues.

McKinsey Quarterly Health Care page
(www.mckinseyquarterly.com/category_editor.aspx?L2=12&srid=6)
In-depth analysis of health care business issues.

MedCareers (www.medcareers.com)
Medical careers website.

Modernhealthcare.com (www.modernhealthcare.com)
Site run by Crain Communications, a business publisher, covering health care industry news and issues.

New England Journal of Medicine (http://content.nejm.org/)
The online presence of the noted medical journal.

The Health Care Blog (www.thehealthcareblog.com)
Must-read blog by industry consultant Matthew Holt.

The Healthcare IT Guy (www.healthcareguy.com)
Blog by a longtime health care–IT professional.

BOOKS

A Brief History of Disease, Science, and Medicine

This book covers everything from prehistoric times to the present day, with an emphasis on 20th century developments.

Michael Kennedy (Asklepiad Press, 2004)

Beyond Managed Care: How Consumers and Technology Are Changing the Future of Health Care

A look at how things like the Internet and clinical information technology are changing the shape of the health care industry.

Dean C. Coddington, Elizabeth A. Fischer, Keith D. Moore, Richard L. Clarke (Jossey-Bass, 2000)

The Cambridge Illustrated History of Medicine

A study of medical history in a variety of cultures.

Edited by Roy Porter (Cambridge University Press, 2001)

The Care of Strangers: The Rise of America's Hospital System

The history and evolution of hospitals in the United States.

Charles E. Rosenberg (The Johns Hopkins University Press, 1995)

The Economic Evolution of American Health Care: From Marcus Welby to Managed Care

An in-depth look at the historical evolution of health care technology and economics.

David Dranove (Princeton University Press, 2002)

Healthwise Handbook

Kaiser Permanente's famous book on preventative medicine and self-care, which is given to all new members. Based on the philosophy that educated people are much better patients, this book is a health care how-to guide for the whole family.

Healthwise, Inc., Boise, ID, 2003

Managed Care: What It Is and How It Works (Second Edition)

A look at the history and current state of managed care.

Peter R. Kongstvedt (Aspen Publishers, 2003)

Medicare's Midlife Crisis

All about Medicare's history, administration, and effects on patients and society.

Sue A. Blevins (Cato Institute, 2001)

HR Consulting Resources

The American Society of Training and Development (www.astd.org)
Organization for training- and development-focused HR folks.

Benefits & Compensation Solutions (http://bcsolutionsmag.com/)
News and information for benefits and compensation pros.

Human Resources @ the University of Arizona
(www.hr.arizona.edu/HRadmin/HRprofs/index.php)
Links to tons of HR-related websites.

Human Resource Executive (www.hreonline.com/HRE/index.jsp)
News and information for high-level HR pros.

The International Association for Human Resource Management (www.ihrim.org)
Website of the International Association for HR Information Management.

Society for Human Resource Management (www.shrm.org)
Comprehensive HR-related resources.

Workforce Management (www.workforce.com)
News and features for HR pros.

BOOKS

Effective Succession Planning

A look at all the issues involved in maintaining or improving organizational performance when key employees move on.
William J. Rothwell (AMACOM, 2005)

How Leaders Build Value

Includes information on how human capital contributes to shareholder value.

Norm Smallwood and Dave Ulrich (John Wiley & Sons, 2006)

HR Value Proposition

A look at the ins and outs of how HR creates value.

Dave Ulrich and Wayne Brockbank (Harvard Business School Press, 2005)

Magic Numbers for Human Resource Managers

A look at a variety of metrics that can contribute to HR management.

Hugh Bucknall and Wei Zheng (John Wiley & Sons, 2005)

The New American Workplace

An overview of critical HR issues.

Edward E. Lawler, III and James O'Toole (Palgrave MacMillian, 2006)

Proving the Value of HR

A look at how to calculate return on investment (ROI) for the HR function.

Jack J. Phillips, Ph.D., and Patricia Pulliam Phillips, Ph.D. (SHRM, 2005)

Rethinking Strategic Compensation

All about attracting, motivating, and retaining employees via compensation.

Brent Longnecker (CCH, 2004)

Roadmap to Diversity, Inclusion, and High Performance

An overview of how to implement diversity initiatives.

William A. Guillory (Innovations International, Inc, 2004)

Technology Consulting Resources

ONLINE RESOURCES

CNET (www.cnet.com)
News, product reviews, downloads, and more.

eWEEK (www.eweek.com)
Enterprise technology news and reviews.

Slashdot.org (http://slashdot.org/)
"News for nerds. Stuff that matters."

Wired News (www.wired.com)
All the latest from the wonderful world of technology.

ZDNet (www.zdnet.com)
"Where technology means business."

BOOKS

A Guide to the Project Management Body of Knowledge

The standard for project managers, who are the ones who manage technology development.

Project Management Institute, 2004

The Economics of Information Technology: An Introduction

A look at the economic factors at play in the technology industry.

Hal R. Varian, Joseph Farrell, and Carl Shapiro (Cambridge University Press, 2005)

IT Portfolio Management: Unlocking the Business Value of Technology

An overview of how to manage IT investments.

Bryan Maizlish and Robert Handler (Wiley, 2005)

Product Strategy for High Technology Companies

An in-depth look at high-tech product management.

Michael E. McGrath (McGraw-Hill, 2000)

Weaving the Web

A look at the past, and a preview of the future, by the inventor of the World Wide Web.

Tim Berners-Lee (Collins, 2000)

WetFeet Resources

Visit WetFeet to get help on everything from finding the right firm to acing your case. At www.wetfeet.com, you will find:

- Articles on writing killer cover letters and resumes.

- Tips on putting your best foot forward in your interviews.

- Guides to specific firms.

- An in-depth insider series on how to ace your case interviews.

- A wide range of topical information relevant to your job search.

Consulting Firm Websites

Not only do consulting firm websites provide the "nuts and bolts" information about potential employers (their history, locations, contact information, practice areas, organizational structures, career opportunities, financial information, and the like), they also include a wealth of more detailed information that many job seekers overlook. If you're still hoping to get a sense of the types of consulting projects that each firm actually does, for example, be sure to look for a tab entitled "case studies" or "success stories." Almost all consulting firms include case studies on their website; while client names are often omitted, they're occasionally not (which is helpful if you're also trying to get a sense of the clients that each firm works with). Some websites go into even more granular detail, offering online journals or diaries of consultants at various levels of seniority and working within different industry or function groups. Look for these types of profiles in the careers section of the website. Finally, many smaller, specialized consulting firms offer fairly extensive bios of their consulting professionals. Obviously, you'll never be asked in an interview where a particular consultant got his master's in public policy, but if you're wondering what types of backgrounds a specific firm is looking for, it's worth scanning the qualifications that its current employees bring to the table. This information usually appears under a tab entitled "Meet Our Consultants" or some variation thereof.

In addition, consulting firms regularly publish white papers, studies, and articles as a way to market and promote their services and expertise, educate their clients, and share best practices. If you're interested in a specific firm, take some time to explore its website for information relevant to the practice area you're going into—look for a tab called "publications," "insight," or "thought leadership." Or explore what they've published so that you can speak intelligently about their "thought leadership" in your interview. Here's a selective list of URLs to some of the better publications sections of strategy firms:

Bain: www.bain.com/bainweb/publications/publications_overview.asp
Includes "Best of Bain."

BearingPoint: www.bearingpoint.com/library/index.html
Check out the "Knowledge Repository" organized by industry, solution, and region.

Boston Consulting Group: www.bcg.com/publications/publications_splash.jsp
Cool searchable database lets you find articles by industry, topic, publication type, and by language.

Booz Allen Hamilton: www.strategy-business.com
Booz Allen's well-regarded quarterly, *strategy+business*, is worth a look. Also check out the industry-specific sections (pharmaceutical and medical products; health care).

Deloitte: www.deloitte.com/dtt/section_home/0,2331,sid%253D16695,00.html
Check out the research section and sign up for e-mail alerts.

First Consulting Group: www.fcg.com/Research/FCGNewsletters.aspx
Sign up for e-mail updates and newsletters on trends in the health care industry.

Gartner: www.gartner.com/it/products/research/research_services.jsp
Browse Gartner's research pages to read dozens of focus areas. Some of its content is restricted to registered users.

Hay Group: www.haygroup.com/ww/Research/
Library includes a searchable database on a range of HR topics.

McKinsey & Company: www.mckinsey.com/ideas/
Don't miss the *McKinsey Quarterly*.

Mercer HR Consulting: www.mercerhr.com/knowledgecenter
Allows users to access articles, white papers, and original research on HR topics including employee benefits, executive compensation, and HR communication.

Towers Perrin: www.towersperrin.com/hrservices/

Open the "Publications" tab to access a searchable database of articles and white papers.

Watson Wyatt: www.watsonwyatt.com/research

View summaries of the firm's research reports, technical and policy papers, and current surveys.

WETFEET'S INSIDER GUIDE SERIES

Job Search Guides

Be Your Own Boss

Changing Course, Changing Careers

Finding the Right Career Path

Getting Your Ideal Internship

International MBA Student's Guide to the U.S. Job Search

Job Hunting A to Z: Landing the Job You Want

Killer Consulting Resumes!

Killer Cover Letters & Resumes!

Killer Investment Banking Resumes!

Negotiating Your Salary & Perks

Networking Works!

Interview Guides

Ace Your Case®: Consulting Interviews

Ace Your Case® II: 15 More Consulting Cases

Ace Your Case® III: Practice Makes Perfect

Ace Your Case® IV: The Latest & Greatest

Ace Your Case® V: Return to the Case Interview

Ace Your Case® VI: Mastering the Case Interview

Ace Your Interview!

Beat the Street®: Investment Banking Interviews

Beat the Street® II: I-Banking Interview Practice Guide

Career & Industry Guides

Careers in Accounting

Careers in Advertising & Public Relations

Careers in Asset Management & Retail Brokerage

Careers in Biotech & Pharmaceuticals

Careers in Brand Management

Careers in Consumer Products

Careers in Entertainment & Sports

Careers in Health Care

Careers in Human Resources

Careers in Information Technology

Careers in Investment Banking

Careers in Management Consulting

Careers in Marketing & Market Research

Careers in Nonprofits & Government Agencies

Careers in Real Estate

Careers in Retail

Careers in Sales

Careers in Supply Chain Management

Careers in Venture Capital

Industries & Careers for MBAs

Industries & Careers for Undergrads

Million-Dollar Careers

Specialized Consulting Careers: Health Care, Human Resources, and Information Technology

Company Guides

25 Top Consulting Firms

25 Top Financial Services Firms

Accenture

Bain & Company

Booz Allen Hamilton

Boston Consulting Group

Credit Suisse First Boston

Deloitte Consulting

Deutsche Bank

The Goldman Sachs Group

JPMorgan Chase

McKinsey & Company

Merrill Lynch & Co.

Morgan Stanley

UBS AG

WetFeet in the City Guides

Job Hunting in New York City

Job Hunting in San Francisco